Telling Stories

Telling Stories

TIM BURGESS

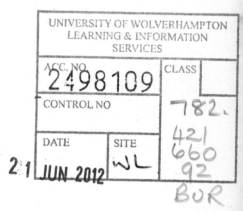

VIKING
an imprint of
PENGUIN BOOKS

VIKING

Published by the Penguin Group
Penguin Books Ltd, 80 Strand, London WC2R ORL, England
Penguin Group (USA) Inc., 375 Hudson Street, New York, New York 10014, USA
Penguin Group (Canada), 90 Eglinton Avenue East, Suite 700, Toronto, Ontario, Canada M4P 2Y3
(a division of Pearson Penguin Canada Inc.)
Penguin Ireland, 25 St Stephen's Green, Dublin 2, Ireland (a division of Penguin Books Ltd)
Penguin Group (Australia), 250 Camberwell Road,
Camberwell, Victoria 3124, Australia (a division of Pearson Australia Group Pty Ltd)
Penguin Books India Pvt Ltd, 11 Community Centre,
Panchsheel Park, New Delhi – 110 017, India
Penguin Group (NZ), 67 Apollo Drive, Rosedale, Auckland 0632, New Zealand
(a division of Pearson New Zealand Ltd)
Penguin Books (South Africa) (Pty) Ltd, Block D, Rosebank Office Park,
181 Jan Smuts Avenue, Parktown North, Gauteng 2193, South Africa

Penguin Books Ltd, Registered Offices: 80 Strand, London WC2R ORL, England

www.penguin.com

First published 2012
001

Copyright © Tim Burgess, 2012

The moral right of the author has been asserted

Set in 12/14.75pt Bembo Book MT Std
Typeset by Jouve (UK), Milton Keynes
Printed in Great Britain by Clays Ltd, St Ives plc

A CIP catalogue record for this book is available from the British Library

HARDBACK ISBN: 978–0–670–92129–4
TRADE PAPERBACK ISBN: 978–0–670–92128–7

www.greenpenguin.co.uk

ALWAYS LEARNING   PEARSON

Contents

Permissions

1. THE BEST BAND IN THE WORLD

When I was asked to write this book, I quickly saw the true potential and scale of the opportunity I'd been given – though it took me a couple of years to ease myself into the driving seat. Like anyone else, my story has been a succession of days that roll into each other, sometimes with direction, sometimes without. Though I've probably had even less of a plan than most.

When I was little, I used to get told off for pushing things too far. Things that seemed to bother other people came quite naturally to me. Like testing whether the goldfish bowl could balance on the edge of the kitchen table.

It didn't.

Or whether I could pedal downhill with no hands and two flat tyres.

I couldn't.

Injuries were painful and trips to the hospital frequent.

Yes, there was blood, but there was also an excitement that came shortly before the disaster. I got a taste for this kind of thing – not exactly danger for the sake of thrill-seeking, more just curiosity.

★ ★ ★

I don't think like a book, in chronological thoughts; it's more a question of ideas invading my head and then inviting others in. I suppose I think more like a magazine or a website: in short bursts, with pictures, charts and lists.

Perhaps it's a mistake to announce this fact at such an early stage. I'm hoping for your sake that everything comes together in a book-like way.

Did they let me do any more after this confession? Are there any more pages?

They did? Cool, let's get started then.

★ ★ ★

Occasionally in your life it seems like outside influences are sent as some kind of guide. You know the kind of thing: some badly behaved kid gets his comeuppance and you take it as a signal to slow down in your own delinquent ways.

At 15 I needed a guide and a path to follow. Something or someone to show me what was possible but with enough interest to engage my erratic temperament (a trait pointed out by Miss Gilchrist on my school report).

I was already of the mind that school wasn't the place where I'd learn the best things to lead me through life, but in fact it was a school trip that first introduced me to the ramshackle parallel worlds of Factory Records and the Haçienda. They were to be my early guides.

For the life of me, I can't now imagine for what reason a bunch of schoolchildren were being led around what would become the epicentre of a musical revolution. It was some time in 1982, and a forward-thinking teacher in the staffroom of Leftwich High School had seen fit, and had it cleared, to take class 5C to an as yet unopened nightclub that would, over the next decade, instruct the world in a new way of doing things.

When the Haçienda opened it showed no signs of being the cultural landmark it would grow into over the next few years. The likes of Graeme Park and Dave Haslam would usher in the house revolution in 1987–8, and with it came a drug called ecstasy and the unifying of a generation that a couple of years earlier had been knocking each other around on the terraces of Old Trafford and Maine Road. But the opening night saw local racist Bernard Manning on the bill, alongside South Bronx, post-punk girl funksters ESG.

So why were we there? I really can't be sure, but I like to think that I was being shown the light. Not that my memories are entirely good. A girl threw up in the doorway. Let's call that something sent from the future, to show me the flavour of things to come, a flavour I couldn't quite put my finger on but one I knew I wasn't fond of.

Anyway, just as some kids would have found their scientific future on our trips to the Jodrell Bank radio telescope or their condiment-calling at the Salt Museum in Northwich – thank God I didn't see the light in there! – everything about the

Haçienda and, in turn, Factory Records captivated me. Little we were shown through school had stirred much emotion in me, but Ben Kelly's futuristic design mothership and Tony Wilson's execution of his take on situationism left me open-mouthed, searching for more. I'd noticed catalogue numbers on the records I owned but they seemed to represent little more than an anti-quated storage system. Factory made them into an art form.

In 1982 everything was different. Everyone was suited up and drinking away their wages in neon and pastel funk dens like Pips and Rotters – this was before any kind of nod towards metro-sexuality. City-centre nightclubs were little more than weekend hunting grounds for a liaison with the opposite sex.

I grew up in a town called Northwich, twenty miles outside Manchester, which was our closest big city. Like many towns close to somewhere casting a cultural shadow, it's safe to say that Northwich didn't offer much to an inquisitive and bored teen-age mind. It was definitely a case of looking to the bright lights of the big city. We heard that the best bands in the world would stop off somewhere near us, party and then leave for the next stage of their world tour.

Famously, there was the Free Trade Hall, where someone had accused Bob Dylan of being 'Judas' when he 'went electric', and he'd replied, 'You're a liar'; where The Sex Pistols had played one of the most iconic gigs in modern music history – OK, it was the Lesser Free Trade Hall, but who's judging? You are? Well, it still counts!; from where Granada regularly broadcast musical milestones into our semi-detached suburban lives.

Punk had made anything seem possible, and the possibilities were starting to become realities at the Haçienda. Bands ruled the roost during the week – groups like Psychic TV and The Jesus and Mary Chain – with worship switching at the week-ends to the DJ booth. So began the rise of the DJ cult.

In the mid to late '80s, I would be there most Tuesday, Thursday, Friday and Saturday nights, making the twenty miles each way pilgrimage from the village of Moulton, near Northwich, to the corner of Whitworth Street West. Any given Tuesday or Thursday night I could pretty much guarantee a ride back home, but on Fridays and Saturdays it was a little more complex. I had to walk, a feat made all the more psychologically daunting by the fact that Northwich isn't even in the same county! The club would close at 2 a.m. and we – always Ronnie, often Frank, and occasionally Chedder and Staggy – would set off down to Deansgate, through Old Trafford, past Manchester United's ground. We'd pass by Morrissey's old house in Stretford, then on through Sale, before arriving at Altrincham train station at about 5 a.m. The first train to Northwich was at 6 o'clock, and we might take it if we had any spare change. From Northwich the final leg was a four-mile walk to Moulton. I would do that at least once most weeks at this time.

I saw a lot of bands at the Haçienda: Death Cult, who were formerly Southern Death Cult and later became The Cult, The Fall, Orange Juice, A Certain Ratio, Section 25. But the most important band I saw there was New Order. They were brilliant at any time, but beyond belief on an otherwise ordinary Tuesday night. Thursday nights saw resident DJ Dave Haslam host the Temperance Club, and although it was thought of as an indie night, the playlists were varied: New Order again, The Rolling Stones, Public Enemy, The Smiths, Mantronix, Sonic Youth, EPMD and The Brilliant Corners. These nights, a really important part of the Haçienda story, are sometimes lost in the all too often rewritten history of the club.

They blazed the trail for the likes of Justin Robertson and The Dust Brothers – Ed and Tom – who began their DJ careers in Manchester but would later change their name and slay the world as The Chemical Brothers.

The Haçienda was like a new friend – recommending music,

always being there for the good times and sometimes the bad. It was there I would witness the changing face of youth culture. Anyone who considered themselves anyone in Manchester's fashion elite would be sprawled on sofas looking cool and being seen.

Another important factor in my musical apprenticeship was my mum's youngest brother, Andrew. That would technically make him my Uncle Andrew, but he never seemed like a traditional uncle, more like an older brother. He was seven years my senior and my first musical guru, the first person I'd come across who was always in a band. He played mostly in Manchester and Bolton, which is where my mum's side of the family are all from, and I would go to as many of his gigs as I could.

He was a vinyl junkie and a gifted guitarist. I remember pictures of Jimmy Page, Marc Bolan and Slade on his wall. He had an inspirational record collection: Hawkwind, Genesis, Jethro Tull, *Tommy*. And he had a few guitars: electric, acoustic and bass. He tried to show me some guitar licks, but that wasn't how he influenced me, really – he just naturally and enthusiastically brought a variety of music into my life. It was listening to his records and seeing the thrill of what being in a band meant that made me take some steps towards being part of this exciting world. I armed myself with a bass guitar, as it seemed a little less complex than the other options.

The U.K. Subs' 'Warhead' was the first song I learned to play, bass in hand, 7-inch brown vinyl on the turntable (a Boots Audio 2000, if I remember rightly). It wasn't the actual playing of the bass that grabbed me so much. I spent a great deal of time just mastering the poses. That was the moment I really decided I wanted to be in a band.

The bass gave way to a classic hairbrush/badminton-racquet/mirror action technique I still use on stage at moments when I am not exactly sure what to do next. I'd seen the world I wanted to be a part of but it still seemed a world away.

Aged 15, I hung around the clothes and record stalls in the underground market in the centre of Manchester where there were some great shops, including the Roxy, where Johnny Marr used to work for future Smiths manager Joe Moss, and a record stall populated almost exclusively by Numanoids, a strange breed of Gary Numan obsessives.

At 16 or 17, when I started my long-lasting love affair with the night life and became almost nocturnal, my uniform was that of the Perry boy, a hybrid of the soul boy and the football hooligan. It made for an odd sight in the streets and on the terraces, as rivals would be dressed in salmon-pink cashmere sweaters and lemon-yellow and pastel-blue tracksuit tops while seemingly attempting to murder each other. I copied my look from my mate Richard Lynch, the cock of the school – I'm not sure how that expression sounds these days, but at the time it was a huge compliment.

My pride and joy was a second-hand navy-blue Fila BJ Mark-2 tracksuit top given to me by my mate Mark Stagg. Staggy had the word BOTH written on his knuckles. At first I actually thought he was bisexual, but no; apparently, while dating a girl called Ruth when he was 14 years old, and being 'absolutely head over heels in love', he felt he simply had to have her name permanently inked on his hand, tattooed for all to see. Sadly she dumped him, so he had it changed to BOTH, as you do. Ironically the dumping was possibly linked to the intense elements of his character that led to the tat in the first place.

I have never been jealous of Staggy's crude four-letter branding, although once in a while I am offered an either/or situation and imagine myself raising Staggy's fist. Or in a parallel world I picture an air hostess offering Mr Stagg the usual choice of 'chicken or fish', to which he silently raises his hand to reveal the legend that demands the two.

I wore polo shirts and gold: a St Christopher, an earring and a krugerrand on my finger. Please take my word that it was 'on trend' at the time, although lately it has become the look of choice for the weed-smoking paternity deniers that populate daytime punch-up TV. Stonewash jeans and Wimbledon trainers completed the look. I've never seen Wimbledon trainers since. They were similar to Adidas Trimm Trab but white with blue and red, and they were easily the coolest footwear ever, alongside black, eight-hole Doc Martens and my classic blue Kickers.

Only me and one other boy, Howard Clarke, had the footwear. He was my partner in crime at that age. Howard owned a 1960s Triumph Vitesse and a GT6, and listened only to '60s pop, not so much The Beatles and The Stones, more The Monkees, The Searchers, Georgie Fame and The Dave Clark Five. He collected '60s theme tunes, too, and had the best leather jacket in the world. I haven't come across him since, but he certainly was a very cool teenager.

At this time my hair was a homage to – or rip off of – Bernard Sumner's. I have always been a fan of the follicles, and it's been an outward expression of my inner self since I saw a picture of Julie Driscoll on my mum's cabinet. I have been told a time or two that people have gone into the hairdresser's clutching a picture of me. As many girls as boys, I'm happy to say.

If these times can concentrate into one moment, like the alignment of the planets, it was 7 March 1983 and the release of New Order's 'Blue Monday'. I had no idea 'Blue Monday' belonged aesthetically to New York: I just thought it was right out of Manchester. I instantly became a huge fan because New Order took me somewhere else, onto what I considered a more serious level of musical consciousness. I realized music could be intelligent.

★ ★ ★

If you want to trace it, like some kind of musical genealogy, it goes all the way back to 1972. The first record I ever bought was Jimmy Osmond's 'Long-haired Lover from Liverpool', not such a misdemeanour if you consider that I was only 5 years old. From there, it was Slade and The Bay City Rollers. I particularly noticed the effect that The Bay City Rollers had on the girls at Moulton County Primary School; it seemed like almost overnight everything turned tartan. Next I remember turning my attention to Thin Lizzy after watching them on *Top of the Pops*. I loved the fact that Phil Lynott had an earring. In his left ear one week, and his right ear the next. Disgruntled dads across the land would claim it was a subliminal, subversive, sexuality statement.

Top of the Pops was a yardstick and lifechanger for each generation and each style of music for a couple of decades. Many a Friday morning would see the youth of Britain adopting a sound or look only seen around 7.30 the previous evening. From Queen to Wham to Dexy's, to the coupling of The Stone Roses and The Happy Mondays on possibly the most iconic edition in its history. My watershed moment came when The Vibrators played 'Automatic Lover'. I declared myself a punk the next day at school and from then on I was on my path towards wherever it was I was going!

Top of the Pops mapped my every musical phase, from glam through early punk, through two-tone, New Wave and New Romantic, despite often being fronted by grinning goons like Dave Lee Travis, Mike Read and Pat Sharp. It also introduced us to the good guys, like Janice Long, John Peel, Kenny Everett and Jimmy Savile. I was too young to remember when I first saw it, and I'm too kind to dwell on the day it limped out of existence. It just always seemed to be there.

But outside the mainstream that the TV chart rundown was giving me, I was developing a hunger for something extra. And knocking around with people who I considered much more sophisticated in their music taste gave me the chance to find it. While I was listening to bands like Discharge, Crass, Blitz, Vice Squad and Chron Gen, all of whom I still love, they were listening to Kraftwerk, Scritti Politti, Throbbing Gristle and Joy Division. I wanted to hang up my studded leather jacket and bleached jeans and change into Harrington, loafers and Sta-prest.

The year was 1983, and New Order's *Power, Corruption and Lies* was permanently on the turntable. New Order were ever-present, and I wanted to know all I could find out about them. The geekier side of my personality became a scrapbook junkie. I bought everything connected to them.

I had a vivid imagination and I even used to write up fictitious set-lists for imaginary gigs. I bought all the music magazines and cut out all the articles about them in *Sounds*, *NME* and *Smash Hits*.

They defied convention, opting for abstract images and anything but their faces on their Peter Saville sleeves. And their songs didn't even mention their titles. New Order were everywhere. In my room. In my head.

I found *The New Order Scrapbook* for sale in a small ad in the *Melody Maker*. I was encouraged and relieved that there were other people out there like me. At the front of the book there was a photographic discography featuring all their releases, including bootlegs, and a list of every interview the band had done up to this point, the summer of 1983. Plus there was a whole section on Joy Division and Ian Curtis. Ian was the pinnacle of cool with the people I was trying to be like, but all I knew was that he'd died in 1980. I wanted to find out more about him.

Outside my new-found cool friends, who were the Northwich wine bar and regatta crew, I was still hanging around with the old gang. We were 16, slightly aimless but inquisitive.

We did a ouija board one evening round at Janet Moore's, and naturally we asked to contact a spirit. The only people I knew on 'the other side' were my paternal grandfather, my much-missed nan and a recently deceased school caretaker. I wanted to contact someone more exciting.

The glass skidded around the letters and I asked if 'the spirit' knew Ian Curtis. The glass took off, spelling out Y–E–S.

'How?' I replied, with a mixture of giddiness and fear.

'I share a room with him!'

I wanted to challenge whatever force we were talking to, to prove its credentials. 'If you share a room with Ian Curtis, you'll know which band he was in.'

The glass responded slowly: J–O–Y–4–T–I–M

Looking back and not wishing to belittle the excitement of my younger self, I think the naivety of those in contact with the spirit world was revealed by the fact that the eternal afterlife involved roommates, a situation uncannily similar to many of our domestic set-ups at that time! I'm a little less naive now than I was then, though only lately, and not necessarily for the better.

Anyway, back to the tangible world of my new scrapbook and its listing of tours that had taken place in Australia, New Zealand and America. It had never crossed my mind that bands played in such exotic places. I had got to grips with the badminton-racquet posing, and now world travel sat high on my agenda. This was a job I had my sights set on.

I began to see the bands I liked more and more on TV. It was a great time for music, but New Order were special and there was the bonus that they were from near where I lived. They were my local heroes, and I was watching them grow. This incredible music was being made by four people, three men and one woman, two of whom were from Salford, where I was born, and two from Cheshire, which is where I was growing up. For the first time, that job with no application form seemed like it might be attainable. And on top of all this New Order managed to make the biggest-selling 12-inch record of all time.

In my mind there was always the possibility of running into them, and a little background knowledge suggested that the Haçienda would be the most likely place for this to happen. I became a regular. In time, it would become the hippest club in the world.

Tony Wilson spoke on behalf of the band, or rather he spoke instead of the band. Tony was a great orator, who loved the sound of his own voice. He had a lot to say and they had very little. The perfect team. He was their frontman in a lot of ways.

Everything about the band appealed to me: Peter Saville's iconic sleeves, the catalogue numbers, the aloofness and their ever-changing manifestos, and the fact that Tony Wilson read the news on TV to me while I was having my tea. Their ownership of the coolest club imaginable was the icing on the cake.

There was one more thing which tied it all together. My mum used to work in a newsagent's in our village, and Tony Wilson and Alan Erasmus, who was one of the partners of Factory Records, were regular customers. My mum would chat with them, Alan mostly. She said he was very charming. She told him she had a son who was really into music. One day Alan gave my mum a badge, an enamel beauty, a blue and yellow rectangle with three letters and two numbers: Fac 51.

From Alan, to my mum, to me.

As my mum handed me the badge my mind was awash with thoughts. Was this the best thing I'd ever owned? Was I part of the gang? Did they even know who I was? Did this mean I'd made it?

And why did my own mother have more connections with the music business than I did?

Later in the week, when Alan came back to the shop, she told him how excited and grateful I was.

For my 16th birthday, I received copies of *Low-Life* (Fact 100) signed by New Order, a 'Confusion' (Fac 93) 12-inch white label, The Durutti Column's *LC* (Fact 44) and a 12-inch version of 'Lips That Would Kiss', which was on Factory Benelux – the catalogue number was FBN 2.

From that point on I collected everything that was on Factory, not so much as a geek thing, more as a taste thing. I knew that the records Factory were putting out were at best genius and at worst extremely interesting. I was falling in love with the label – and with the story regarding my mum's acquaintance with Alan Erasmus. I was now part of the whole thing. According to me anyway.

On that birthday I went for a meal with my mum, dad and sister, and there was an extra place setting. I later found out it was meant for Alan, but he never showed up. He wrote me a letter apologizing for 'his mad existence' and dropped off even more records. Maybe he didn't realize he totally had me from the moment he gave me the badge.

And maybe I joined a band just to see if he was telling the truth about the mad existence.

Although I had still never met Alan I received an invitation to the Haçienda for a live special of my favourite TV show, *The Tube*. The show was to include The Factory All-Stars, various artists on the Factory Records roster including Donald Johnson, Bernard Sumner, 52nd Street, Mike Pickering, Vinni Reilly, Section 25, Marcel King and The Wake.

Oh, and Madonna, making her British TV debut.

The invitation was for Friday, 27 January 1984. On Thursday, I was in the back seat of a mate's car that hit a lamp post on the corner of Leftwich Green on our way back from a night out in Northwich. I'm not sure whether I broke my ankle on impact or when I jumped out of the rear window as the car was filling up with smoke. But on the Friday morning I was on crutches, in shorts and in plaster. I just couldn't face the show.

Once fully recovered I told myself I would never miss out on anything again, even if I had to go to gigs on my own. I kept my promise to myself and went to London to see New Order at Heaven in August 1984 and at the Woolwich Coronet in April 1987.

I was also at the Macclesfield Leisure Centre, one of their most legendary gigs, in April 1985. I remember Hooky hitting someone over the head with his bass as a fight broke out at the front. I also remember giving Hooky a hug in the car park at Warrington's Spectrum Arena!

Despite their contrary marketing ways, New Order proved that having good songs was the key. This led to a headline slot on the main stage at the 1987 Glastonbury festival. I remember Bernard smashing his guitar and putting it through his amp during the encore – a cover of 'Sister Ray' by the Velvet Underground. Joy Division used to play it, and their live version is on side 2 of the album *Still*.

Andy Liddle was New Order's lighting guy, and on the BBC recording of the Glastonbury show you can hear Bernard growl some strobe command over the microphone, leading to an overwhelming laser spectacle. Andy now does the lights for The Charlatans. As I once collected their records, we now appear to be collecting New Order crew: Dian Barton, Oz, Roger Lyons and the much-missed Rex Sargeant.

New Order live was no easy ride. One minute they were electrifying and self-assured, the next thrillingly confused. They were working with very advanced, state of the art technology which could and would go wrong at any second. Remember, at this time a calculator was the size of an iPad and could perform little more than the basic + − ÷ × operations, and they had early versions of drum machines, sequencers and samplers which were wheeled on stage resembling techno fridges. They and their technicians were learning from scratch in the public eye, while enjoying a cocktail in summery clothes: shorts and t-shirts for Bernard, flowery dresses for Gillian.

Charming, aloof, casual and random, New Order were unpredictable and just like life. That's why I liked them. You had absolutely no idea what to expect, from sheer ethereal beauty to audience brawling. They had it all. They were shiny but not polished, free-form within the unidentified box they had plonked themselves in.

★ ★ ★

According to my mum, I always wanted to be involved in music. Trouble is, I had a tendency to say one thing one minute, and then forget about it the next. My mum was also known to say that I was going to be a spaceman, as I was fascinated by the moon. I suppose it's true though that from an early age I did want to be involved in music, but then again so did everybody else.

I was surprisingly happy working in an office, sticking down envelopes, photocopying, filing and losing stuff. I was like Jimmy from *Quadrophenia*, without the uppers and the angst.

I began a job at ICI when I was 16. I was a mail-delivery boy, delivering the post by bike to the various drop-off points around the chemical factory in Winnington. All of this was made less mundane by my Sony Walkman, the original personal audio cassette player. I would make compilation tapes at home in the evening then listen to them all day at work. The cassettes had to be just so.

I must have been preparing myself for a life in the studio as I loved sitting at home, drinking black coffee and dreaming about a wider audience. I would serenade girlfriends with the compilations, documenting cool times together.

I learned how to drive while at ICI. They gave me free lessons and a free test. I passed first time, and my life simply got a tiny bit better. I got myself a 1974 Triumph Dolomite in British racing green with a white boot. The pile of tapes in the passenger seat featured the sounds of The Style Council, The Cure, Everything But The Girl, REM, The B-52s, Fad Gadget, Aztec Camera, Orange Juice, ACR, The Meteors, Prefab Sprout, Scritti Politti . . .

I had the car, I had the music, and as vain as it may seem my hair was next on my list of priorities. Hey, I was 17 and I was sharp.

Only later did I get serious. At this point, I had an ever-growing fringe and an update on the short back and sides, courtesy of Dean Sutton of Suttons' Unisex hairdressers, Northwich. Dean used to cut my hair, but I would source the inspiration from record sleeves or magazines, or give him a hastily described style I'd seen on someone at a gig or in the street.

I had a few variations featuring elements of the flicker, the flattop and the moptop. I had a Specials-era 'Terry Hall' cut and a Fun Boy Three-era 'Terry Hall' cut. Dean advised drawing the line at a 'Grace Jones' silver wedge-head look. Looking back I think I need to thank Dean for refusing to take part in that one.

A classic Sutton cut was the one you see in the 'Only One I Know' video. I had been having that style for a good few months before word filtered back that people were going in the barber's asking for a 'Tim Burgess'.

Thursday was pay day, and with that tradition came my own tradition – a weekly trip to the record shop, Omega Records, owned by our future manager, Steve Harrison. I would spend nearly all of my £40 wages, keeping back the minimum amount of board I could hand over to my mum. This was roughly half of what my dad thought I was paying.

I would ride my bike back home one-handed, the other hand firmly gripping the sweet-smelling heavy vinyls I had just bought. Then upstairs till late with my headphones on, listening with keen ears till falling asleep, my dreams becoming videos to the songs I'd just bought.

And then Friday night's soundtrack was listened to with windows and doors open and a hastily grabbed bath during the advert break of *The Tube*. *The Tube* was hosted by Jools Holland and Paula Yates, the bloke you wanted to be and the girl you wanted to go out with, except they were in your living room and talking about the things that ruled your life.

As well as being a music tastemaker, *The Tube* was the first show to feature A Certain Ratio in their sexy shorts. I was smitten, I'd been bitten. *The Tube* would give me a start on next week's list for my splurge at Omega Records. The likes of New Model Army, The Associates, The Cocteau Twins, Devine, The Gun Club, Scraping Foetus Off the Wheel, SPK and Wall of Voodoo. As The Charlatans' manager, Steve Harrison would eventually be earning 20 per cent of the band's income, but at this time in his shop he was taking around 80 per cent of my weekly earnings, which I would eagerly hand over on pay day.

Steve was a genuine music fanatic. He was ten years older than me, a veteran from the era of Eric's in Liverpool and the Electric Circus in Manchester. He was full of stories from those days; fortunately, I could listen to his stories all day long – and I often did. Steve had seen Joy Division and Wire, which was enough to seal the deal on our friendship.

When he became the manager of The Charlatans, before I joined, Steve got them a few gigs.

Would it be inappropriate to say that they weren't fully formed yet as a band? Yes, maybe it would, so I won't. I'll try another way. Let's just say that they weren't quite there yet as a band.

But hey, I don't want to be too harsh. After all, I was in a not fully perfect band myself then, bequiffed and doing cover versions.

The Charlatans' frontman was Baz Ketley, though it was obvious to me that Martin Blunt, their bass player, was at the helm. He'd been in a couple of bands before, most notably the mod band Makin' Time, who I had liked. When Makin' Time broke up I was interested in what each of them was going to do next.

My attention was caught by Martin, who, along with Makin' Time frontwoman Fay Hallam and The Prisoners' guitarist, had formed a band called The Gifthorses, which also featured Keith Moon-fanatic, phenomenal powerhouse drummer and West Midlands nutcase Jon Brookes.

One single and a German tour later the band split.

Martin and Jon now formed the backbone of The Charlatans. Years later, after our first show at the Brixton Academy, someone pointed out that they were reminiscent of the Mighty Stax rhythm section. The Brummie MGs. What they needed now was their Booker T.

Around this time the best Hammond organ player in the West Midlands was a character by the name of Rob Collins, who could be regularly seen lugging his X-5 around with local pub outfit The Rembrandts. (Not the LA band who recorded the theme tune to *Friends*. Nope, this lot were firmly rooted in the Bloxwich underground music scene.)

Martin's vision was to be in a band like his heroes, The Prisoners. Their sound was based around the Hammond organ, and Martin was listening out for the right person for The Charlatans. Admittedly the West Midlands music scene wasn't awash with masters of such a specialist instrument, which is way more complicated to play than a regular keyboard. Jon Brookes had played in a band with Rob and suggested he join them – Martin was keen, although Rob's reputation as a bit of a loose cannon had preceded him, making Martin also a little wary. He had already been charged with a couple of assaults, reportedly only minor pub scrapes or chipshop-queue misunderstandings and always with a willing party. I must say, he was always very protective of me, but though I never saw him set out to start anything, in truth I never saw him duck out either.

This was Rob. He became the newest member of The Charlatans.

Baz Ketley had had various levels of success with ex-members of both The Bureau and Dexy's Midnight Runners. He was a gifted singer songwriter who was admired in local circles and seemed like a dead cert. Martin invited him to write some songs with them, and Baz became the singer and guitarist in the band.

So The Charlatans now consisted of Martin Blunt on bass, Jon Brookes drums, Rob Collins keyboards and Baz Ketley guitar and vocals.

This was The Charlatans Mk 1. They had a manager, they had a place to rehearse, and they had songs.

Martin retained his mod credentials. Jon had a floppy fringe and reliable blue and white striped t-shirts. Baz sported spikey hair and 501s. Rob had a black leather car coat, faded jeans with ripped knees and . . . a moustache, grown unannounced. It was a style last seen on one of Dexy's Midnight Runners circa 'Geno', 1980. I imagine he was thinking a bit Clark Gable, while everyone else was thinking *Coronation Street*'s long-serving grease monkey, Kevin Webster.

Nobody at this early stage knew him well enough, or perhaps was brave enough, to say that, though none of them was really keen on it. It was an unwelcome feature in the group. Steve backed out of telling him, claiming it was out of his managerial jurisdiction.

It was Martin who eventually took it into his own hands and did something about it, although in an unconventional and roundabout way. He had been choosing photos for the band's very first publicity shot. He picked his favourite, but directly before handing it to Steve he made one small amendment. With a swipe of Tippex the moustache was gone, replaced by a mysterious and obvious white brush stroke on Rob's upper lip. When Rob saw it, he was at first furious, but he either took a shine to his new look or was embarrassed by the silent censorship. Shortly afterwards the moustache was no more and Rob's top lip matched the one in the photo.

Steve Harrison invited me to see the band opening for The Stone Roses. I still don't know if there was an ulterior motive to his actions or whether he was simply proud of his new signings. The Stone Roses were in the early stages of being the band that they were about to become. They were hitting a groove after some line-up and image changes. Mani had just joined and they were exorcizing their Goth beginnings with their new-found Byrdsian jangle. They were now sounding a little like the bands that had recently been lumped together and touted as 'The Paisley Underground', a predominantly LA-based scene made up of bands like Rain Parade (check out 'Talking in My Sleep' and 'You Are My Friend'), The Three o'Clock, Dream Syndicate and Green on Red, as championed by Manchester DJ Tony Michaelides, otherwise known as Tony the Greek.

The Roses' manager, Gareth Evans, owned a club called the International on the corner of Anson Road and Dickenson Road in Longsight (now a Turkish supermarket called Venus Foods, should you be driving past). The venue subsequently became known as International 1 after he opened International 2 on a much bigger site on Plymouth Grove in Rusholme.

Gareth was a manager/club owner/entrepreneur, at a point somewhere between Peter Grant and Ron Atkinson. Like many entrepreneurs, some of his skills in his chosen field were limited. His musical knowledge wasn't great, and some would say he didn't know what he had in The Stone Roses. But someone somewhere, maybe him, knew how to book a good gig. His venues hosted some of the most iconic shows ever put on in Manchester: The Pixies, De La Soul, The Housemartins, Jane's Addiction, Suicide, James, The Inspiral Carpets, The Ramones.

And, on multiple occasions, The Stone Roses.

Gareth became friends with Steve Harrison through Steve's record shop. And, because he needed musical affirmation, Gareth would ask whether his band was any good. To which Steve would duly reply, 'Gareth, they are the best band in the world!' Steve ended up booking some of the Stone Roses gigs outside Manchester, venues like Nottingham Trent Polytechnic, Dudley J.B.'s and Warrington Legends, and he recommended The Charlatans as the support band.

★ ★ ★

International 2, 6 May 1989

Steve and I walked through the foyer and into the gig. Sweaty bodies dressed in the daisy age long-sleeved t-shirts and loose-fit coolness of the day mixed with regular indie kids and girls. Lots of girls.

Steve confided in me that there was trouble on the horizon, Charlatans-wise. Apparently, Baz was the source of these difficulties.

We made our way through the mass of bodies and ended up about thirty rows from the front, just about the time that The Charlatans hit the stage and kicked off with 'Hey! Teen'. Jon led, with a Ringo-inspired, all-out, heads-down drum loop. The audience began to move to the beat, and seemed to realize that this was going to be more than your average local filler support slot.

We were standing nearest to Rob, who was fast becoming the focal point. Stage right, Martin epitomized the solid bass-playing cool famously trademarked by John Entwistle of The Who. Front and centre was the figure of Baz, a tough guy in black denim wielding a Fender Telecaster. His stage persona came across like someone who idolized The Clash when the world was shifting over to something a little more West Coast than Westway.

Thinking about that gig now is like having an out-of-body experience, watching somebody play me in a film where I was set to play the ghost of someone else before they'd actually left us.

I might not be putting this very well, but let's just say time was running out for Baz.

They went through their handful of songs, a couple of which I had heard on demos that Steve had played in the car. They also did a cover version of Department S's 'Is Vic There?' However, the most exciting and memorable part of the set for me was the end section of the final song, a long sprawling psychedelic freakout called 'Nothing's Left', in which Rob really came to the fore. You could see his feet working as fast as his hands through the chrome bumper stand, which gave the impression that the Hammond was levitating in front of him. He was tearing up and down the keyboard, punching, kicking and wrestling out what would become the axis of The Charlatans' sound, leading to the climax of Jon kicking over his beloved drum kit.

Up till that point I had been a little surprised that, while Martin had got his wish for a Hammond-heavy band, it wasn't until the final section of the last song that the organ took the lead. Rob literally pulled out all the drawbars. Looking back now, I can see that the band were finding their feet and heading towards a new world – taking steps towards writing songs like

'Indian Rope', 'Everything Changed' and the set-closing magnum opus, 'Sproston Green'.

The band left the stage having caught the interest of about a third of the audience. Ian Brown came on stage playing with a yo-yo and the whole crowd erupted. The Stone Roses were on their way.

★ ★ ★

As fate would have it, it would be Baz who I would get on with best. He had no idea that I was about to get his job, but then again neither did I. I wasn't aware that the rest of the band were looking beyond Baz for their future.

After the gig I tried to keep my thoughts to myself. But as he was driving me home Steve asked me what I'd made of the band's performance. He really wanted to know, and since I didn't appreciate at the time that this was some kind of unorthodox job interview, I offered my opinion a little bit tentatively.

He agreed with me, but told me I was never allowed to tell anyone what he and I had just decided: the band wouldn't fulfil their potential with Baz there.

Oops, I've let the cat out of the bag.

I hope, after all this time, that that's no major revelation. Martin, Rob and Jon didn't really like where they were going musically, but Baz was their singer, guitarist and songwriter. They loved The Prisoners, The Stone Roses and the club sounds coming from Detroit and Chicago.

It was 1989 and the Haçienda had morphed from cavernous indie financial drain to sell-out ecstasy-fuelled clubbing vanguard. The yardstick for me was New Order, fresh back from Ibiza holding the masters for their new album. The entire world had changed in a matter of months.

By this stage I was forming a really tight bond with Steve Harrison, spending more and more time in his record shop. So when he booked The Charlatans to play at Northwich Vics' club, I asked if my band, The Electric Crayon Set, could open.

I had tried to get Steve down to look at my band before, but he had never shown up. I was convinced he didn't like us, but I wanted him to at least sell our record in his shop. I secretly wanted him to manage us, but anyway he agreed to let us support on this occasion. Rob watched The Electric Crayon Set, and although he wasn't keen on the band itself he saw something in me. The rest of The Charlatans just took a cursory glance.

I think we did OK – I enjoyed myself, anyway.

I was standing in the front row when The Charlatans themselves came on stage and I found myself singing along to a couple of their songs. When it got to their encore, Martin gestured for me to get up and sing into his mic. Thus emerged The Charlatans Mk 2. Very short-lived – one song – but a highly important transitional line-up.

Rob later told me that he was sure he had found The Charlatans' new singer that night: me. I was doing cool and aloof at the time so didn't really respond, but inside I was dancing.

The next obvious step was to tell Baz.

Martin was the de facto leader, and he decided straws would be drawn, as nobody really wanted the job of informing Baz of his fate. They were all scared of him, except perhaps Rob; he just pretended he was scared of him. It was an unpleasant job which nobody wanted to do.

Martin drew first and it was evident that there wouldn't be any shorter straws, as Martin had cut them up himself. It broke the tension, but increased the look of worry on Martin's face.

The story goes that Martin knocked on Baz's door and said to him, 'Hi-ya, mate, can I talk to you about something for a second?' To which Baz replied, 'Yeah, sure. I got something I want to tell you too.'

Baz went first. 'Listen, Martin, I've been thinking that I should leave the band.'

Martin went quiet. 'Oh! Sorry to hear about that, mate, but if you've thought long and hard about it and you've made your decision, me and the lads will have to accept it.'

Baz asked Martin what he'd been planning to say. 'Nothing, really, I was just going to ask you a few questions about Steve and a few bits and bobs about the band – but it doesn't really matter now.' And with that he was off the hook.

They were now a singerless, guitarless three-piece. Through Steve they arranged for me to go to their rehearsal room to sing. The term 'audition' sounds a little too formal; I already knew them well, and, while I was very aware of their ambition, this getting together was more about hanging out and seeing where it would go, seeing if I could do it – not a shot-in-the-dark *Melody Maker* small ad.

They were also going to try out a new guitarist called Jon Baker, from Walsall psych band Liquidy Egg Box. They moved fast and had already lined up a rehearsal for us both that weekend.

They were doing exactly what I had hoped.

They sounded like Brian Auger and The Trinity mixed with The Chocolate Watch Band. And Jon Baker looked like a cross between Brian Jones and Graham Day from The Prisoners, so much so that for some reason the credits for 'The Only One I Know' refer to him as Jon Day. Perhaps a homage? Perhaps he was still signing on?

This first meeting was in Wednesbury, on a Sunday in late May 1989. Steve drove me there in his black Mercedes. I kept it simple and cool with just a touch of weird: a white t-shirt and dark-blue girls' flared jeans, with blue Kickers.

My mind was churning. Had they liked me fronting the Crayons? Was I the only candidate? And would I take the job if I was offered it?

It was a secret meet-up, and I had feelings of guilt because The Electric Crayon Set, who were now just called The Electric Crayons, were about to release their debut single, 'Hip Shake Junkie' c/w 'Happy to be Hated'.

I asked Steve exactly what the band were thinking, as everything seemed to be up in the air, but he was quite cagey. Once we were there, I met the band and was introduced to their new guitarist, Jon, who had spent the previous couple of days learning the songs.

We did a cover of 'Lucifer Sam' by Pink Floyd, and on the second run-through Martin said to me, 'Try singing it this time, Tim.' Blunt by name, blunt by nature, but I got what he said. And so began a band and a set of relationships where everybody felt confident and comfortable enough to say what they thought.

I had myself down as more of a frontman than a singer, and in The Electric Crayons I had been doing my best Iggy-meets-Jim-Morrison impersonation: no shirt, writhing across the stage, shouting and screaming along to 'LA Woman', Led Zep's 'Houses of the Holy' and The Stooges' smash 'I Wanna Be Your Dog', as well as a couple of our own songs, so I had lost myself in that style. But, as ever, I immersed myself in my surroundings, and during the next run-through I sang 'Lucifer Sam' as softly and with as much fragility as I could. I imagined Syd Barrett whispering in my ear. Martin looked surprised and Rob looked happy, but truthfully I was more surprised than Martin and happier than Rob!

Then we did a couple of Charlatans songs, written by Baz and still considered part of their set. First the sprawling Hammond-jam 'Nothing's Left', which had been the stand-out track at the

Roses gig, and also the song I'd sung backing vocals on at the Vics' club. Then 'Hey! Teen' – my favourite of theirs, with its beat reminiscent of 'Tomorrow Never Knows'. The only trouble was, I had no emotional connection to the lyrics. They had no real meaning for me, and I found it hard to sing as someone else. I wanted to sing about my world, fifty miles away, a world that took in *Brighton Rock*, Calvin and Hobbes, the West Coast, dinosaurs, Anthony Burgess, *Letter to Brezhnev*, Felt, Ken Loach, Ken Russell, Kenny Everett, and the thousand and one things that were invading my senses each day.

They then played two instrumentals, one directly after another, and I made up the melodies then and there, inventing the words on the spot, singing about bad girls and saying goodbye. It was what you might call A Moment. A moment of pure magic. It was effortless and spontaneous. This was it. This is what I had been waiting for. I had been thrown in at the deep end, and this was the sound of me emerging drenched but euphoric.

Song #1

I sang really softly. It was slow and psychedelic. It was the first time I had ever really used my own voice. After Martin passed me a note that read, 'Don't bring me flowers, I am not dead,' I took it as a given that we were in this together. We called the song 'Flower', and I knew straight away that we were on to something good. Just over a year later it would be on our debut album.

I wasn't really sure whether the band were considering anyone else at the time, I certainly didn't see anybody else in the queue. I know Steve and Rob were already convinced that I was the man for the job, but it's fair to say that Martin and Jon Brookes needed some persuading.

Song #2

If Song #1 was 'Flower', the second would become 'Always in Mind' — an early live favourite that never made the album but did eventually appear on a John Peel Session.

To me this was the kind of song that Rob was made for.

And it felt like the best music I had ever heard in my life.

We went for a drink and they told me quite matter of factly that I was now in The Charlatans. The Charlatans Mk 3.

★ ★ ★

Now I was in the band I felt more comfortable. The others seemed to feel the same and we all opened up, sharing ideas, tapes and recommendations.

I was into The Rolling Stones' 'Child of the Moon' and Orange Lemon's 'Dreams of Santa Anna'. One is Chicago house, the other a B-side of a 1967 single. Quite diverse, but we were looking for the point where they crossed. Jon Brookes threw in 'Talk Talk' while Jon Baker contributed Diana Ross and the Supremes' 'You Keep Me Hanging On' and Dionne Warwick's 'Do You Know the Way to San Jose?', as well as all things Roky Erickson. Martin brought The Stranglers and The Move into the mix.

When he was in Makin' Time, Martin like me was inspired by The Prisoners. They were obviously going to be a big influence. Their lead instrument was the Hammond organ pushed through a wah-wah pedal and distorted Leslie speaker, and their singer's voice was close to Steve Marriott or Stevie Winwood.

I travelled to London, Leeds and Bradford to see Kent's greatest exports.

Their albums *In from the Cold* and *The Last Fourfathers* helped define The Charlatans' nascent sound. For reference check out the song 'Find and Seek'. They supplied us with the mod discipline, an aim for a three-minute rush, all done within strict boundaries set up by the likes of Pete Townshend and Steve Marriott, seen through and magnified by Paul Weller and now being meddled with by our various conflicting, complementary musical tastes: punk, acid, prog and even hip-hop.

But if there was a blueprint in Martin's mind for the post-Baz Charlatans it was to splice the looseness of the emerging new sounds of Manchester's Chicago/Detroit-influenced groove with the retro-tightness and primal energy of The Prisoners.

Which is what I think we achieved.

★ ★ ★

There seems to be a dispute as to where exactly the band are from. Because Steve had an office in Northwich, it was decided that that was where the HQ would be. I slept there on boxes of records from time to time, riffling through the stock and asking Steve for permanent loans. But the majority of the band were living in the West Midlands: Walsall, West Bromwich and Wolverhampton. In my opinion we were never a Midlands band. We were always a Manchester band.

Or a Northwich band!

I'm not sure why people get so hung up about it. Didn't Ian Brown say it's not where you're from, it's where you're at?

★ ★ ★

When I first started hanging out with the band, I would spend time writing with Rob and Martin, and I would stay over at Rob's house. The first night I stayed there, he offered me a cigarette and informed me, 'A lot of people say I look like Paul McCartney.' The only link I could think of was a penchant for a now-absent dodgy tash. Maybe there was a similar warmth in the eyes, but I was getting more Rodney Bewes.

He said, 'Maybe we could be the new Lennon and McCartney.' I was thinking we could be the new Likely Lads.

Looking at old photos now, I would say he had more of the look of Stu Sutcliffe. He loved Julian Lennon, probably just because he was the son of John and Cynthia. No disrespect, but he was the only person I've ever heard enthuse about Julian's work.

Rob had been a gravedigger and during our first discussions he seemed to get quite excited about explaining his former line of work.

* * *

I told the band I wanted to write our lyrics, but Martin's defences were up after the odd mauling at the hands of labels and the music business in general. Martin was the most experienced member of the band. He had put out an album with his old group on Stiff Records, which was a major label; after its demise they put another record out under their own steam, without much success. His caution was well founded given his experience. Looking back I can see that we were a bunch of giddy kippers who were just eager to play gigs and make records, but Martin wasn't going to settle for anything short of the right way. He definitely had the best interests of the band at heart, and he thought this was his last chance. At 24, after a glimpse into the world of showbiz, he had had to pick up his old brushes and was working once more as a painter and decorator.

He didn't want the door closing on him again, especially if he was expected to sand it down, undercoat it and gloss it.

Our main aim was to keep at arm's length the kind of boring life mapped out for people like us – not that there was any problem with living that way. From very early on lots of people, particularly young men, kind of pinned their hopes on us. There was a responsibility that came with being in a band. It was a responsibility I had spent so long avoiding, yet it tracked me down and I think I liked it.

The gigs from the outset were a release of anything and everything. People seemed to be able to express themselves in an unbridled way. They were like what I had become accustomed to seeing in the Haçienda, outward displays of affection from people who wouldn't normally do that kind of thing. I had witnessed enough gigs to realize there was something special going on here, and from our very early beginnings we all agreed to look after what came with being The Charlatans.

Meanwhile, The Stone Roses and The Inspiral Carpets were taking their '60s-tinged psychedelic anthems into the indie charts, which was the ultimate aim and meant more than anything at the time. Both bands were selling as many t-shirts as records, to the extent that the Inspirals were effectively being funded by their merchandise sales. They were taking their fans abroad on coach parties organized by the management themselves. These were small, upcoming managers and promoters with big ideas. Steve Harrison, The Inspiral Carpets' manager Anthony Boggiano, The Happy Mondays' manager Nathan McGough and Gareth Evans had lots of differences, but they also shared many qualities. All possessed a Northern spirit making them more like extra members of their respective bands than orthodox managers.

If the rulebook was not being ripped up exactly, it was certainly being thrown around a bit. The Stone Roses were on the verge of something really big. And I mean really big. Their single 'Elephant Stone' was doing well. And I mean really well.

I was into The Happy Mondays. I saw them live in London at a student-union bar in support of their first album. I loved their wild-bunch, chancer attitude. I saw them open for New Order in Birmingham promoting their second LP, *Bummed*, which at that time I thought was the best album of all time. This was 1988, and it's still in my Top 10, though my favourite album of all time changes from day to day.

★ ★ ★

What would I have done if I had not been in a band?

Actually, I was quite happy in my day jobs. I had worked my way through mail-delivery boy, toilet cleaner, labourer and office worker. Yet enjoyable as it was, meeting people and having a relatively responsibility-free existence, I felt I needed more. The only thing that fulfilled me 100 per cent was music. I was happy with my tapes and my coffee, dreaming of making records, but other things called.

I'd been in The Electric Crayon Set with John, Alex and Nick. John was a decent guitarist, an amalgam of Steve Jones and Billy Duffy. Everyone in the band loved Iggy Pop – *New Values* was the record we all agreed on.

I chose the name The Electric Crayon Set from a UK psych compilation album on Bam-Caruso Records; there were some great tracks on it by The Poets, The Flies and The Mark Four, an early incarnation of The Creation. It was John who shortened our name to The Electric Crayons. What he had against those three other letters I will never know.

We recorded a single, paid for by me, and the day I joined The Charlatans was the day it came out. John was furious and saw me as a traitor for leaving them in the lurch. I have never seen anyone so upset. He became my first hater.

The decision to leave The Electric Crayons was an easy one for me, but I knew they would take it really hard. I was certainly Judas for a while in their circles. As soon as The Charlatans' first single, 'Indian Rope', came out, the music weeklies got letters giving me grief, all in the same handwriting and all from the same village.

It would be fair to say that abandoning The Electric Crayons was the first cut-throat decision I ever had to make.

★ ★ ★

My first gig as lead singer of The Charlatans was in Walsall, on Tuesday, 29 August 1989, at a place called the Overstrand. It was Jon Baker's hometown and he was the booker for the club; the entrance fee was £1.50. We had seven original songs at the time: 'Always in Mind', 'Flower', 'Everything Changed', 'Indian Rope', 'You Can Talk to Me', 'Imperial 109' and 'Sproston Green'. I had joined in late May '89, so it had been pretty fast and furious on the songwriting front.

But you know how it is when you first really get into something? You can fully throw yourself into it. We thought we could play our first gig as soon as we wrote our first songs. All we talked about after we'd written those first few was:

When are we gonna play?

Where are we gonna play?

When are we gonna demo?

There was an intense chemistry between us during those first four months. We had all been waiting for this to happen to us. It really was like falling head over heels in love.

The idea/manifesto/only-thing-we-knew was to play live a couple of times and then go and record a demo.

Steve Harrison had sent out letters to record companies with a press release and a clipping from a football fanzine called *Hit the Bar*, who claimed that they had seen us at a private party in Manchester. They hadn't.

It was something me and him had come up with in the stockroom in Steve's new shop in Crewe. There were quotes from me saying, 'The Charlatans are necessary and necessary is something you can't do without,' and 'I think we will be the third biggest band in the world!' These were actually remarks I had made to a drunken girl trying to chat me up at Rob's wedding the week before. (Well, she was either chatting me up or taking the piss; I couldn't tell which with the Brummie accent.) Steve had been listening in and used my quotes on the press release, so it's not like they had never been said. It was just that they had been said by the singer. That's not cheating, is it? Into his mate's fanzine, taken right outta my mouth.

Steve showed me the piece, photocopied it and sent out the press release. I thought it was great! Loog Oldham-inspired.

It worked as well. It got people interested in the band. A word-of-mouth thing started to happen. I soon figured out that if you own a record shop and you have reasonable taste, then people will listen to you.

I guess Steve thought of himself as a kind of Brian Epstein at this point.

We had great songs and a couple of oil lamps, which we used to light the stage. I think they were Rob's. He found them in his neighbour's garage, so they were kind of his.

Anyway, back to the gig. We came on stage to 'Across the Universe' by The Beatles and 'Age of Aquarius' by The Fifth Dimension, lit by those lamps, or psychedelic lights as we liked to think of them, and we had 'Sproston Green' to end the set.

We really thought about every detail: what to wear, the complete look. It was really important, especially to me, Martin and Steve. And it set the tone, set the standard. If we were going to get anywhere, we had to think about the smallest things. The manifesto grew at the same time as the songs.

We wanted to be a psychedelic band, and it had to be Northern. I was the singer: they would be my words, our vision. We felt that people like The Jesus and Mary Chain and the shoe-gazing gang had kept it dark for a long time. We wanted to throw a splash of colour and optimism into our world. Acid house and the pills, and my current love of anything '60s West Coast kaleidoscopic: it all seemed to be coming from the same place.

Our second gig was in Northwich, at the Winnington Rec Social Club on Friday, 1 September. The crowd at the Overstrand had mostly been friends of Jon Baker. There wasn't a stage and there were fewer than fifty people: audience and band as one. The Northwich gig was huge in comparison, I guess because it was close to Manchester and the record shop, or perhaps because the buzz had begun.

It was nuts, kids jumping around everywhere. It was off the hook. I remember Gareth Evans coming to see us and telling us we would go far and saying things like, 'The kids loved it.' This was the first time someone with any kind of clout had said something so positive. It made us believe even more.

The next gig, at J.B.'s in Walsall, maintained the upward trajectory.

I remember the local newspaper saying at the time that anyone interested in what the band were up to should talk to Tim if they saw him wandering about town, and that he wouldn't be hard to miss in his 24-inch flares and his bowl haircut. As the weeks passed, more of my mates took on that look.

* * *

My favourite song in the set was 'Indian Rope', a six-minute Hammond organ solo with a little bit of singing over the top. The singing wasn't the focal point, though, it was just a melody that went along with the beat for a while before the Hammond took on a huge apocalyptic Bob Marley meets Julie Driscoll, Brian Auger and The Trinity stampede.

I sang along with what was being played. The words were not

telling a story, but they were carefully chosen, reflecting and enhancing the mood, the sound and the melody. I also wanted the titles of the songs not necessarily to have any direct reference to the lyrics, to be vibe-inspired. And I wanted to see how far I could push it. For instance, the song 'You Can Talk to Me' I wanted to call 'Choose Time' and 'You're Not Very Well' was originally titled 'Some Friendly'. Our debut single made no reference to Indian rope apart from in the title. I thought if I gave them 'mood titles' it would imbue the songs with an air of mystery.

The words started to write themselves. It wasn't anything as conscious as going direct from my head to my hand, they just seemed to arrive.

We wrote 'Indian Rope' one weekend along with 'The Only One I Know' and 'Sproston Green'. Me lying on the floor, pen in mouth, surrounded by screwed-up pieces of paper containing lyrics that hadn't made the grade;

Rob smoking a Benson and Hedges and fiddling with chord progressions;

Jon Baker taking photographs, our newly appointed roadie, Derek, also taking photographs;

Steve making phone calls and going to the off-licence;

Jon Brookes tapping away and then leaving for his holidays;

Martin playing his bass, chipping in with lyrics and cadging cigarettes from Rob.

There was never just one new song taking shape, there were always a few. 'Sproston Green' was inspired by John Lennon. I had read that once during a recording Lennon had used a megaphone while being spun round in a chair. Inspired, I decided to put a microphone inside a biscuit tin. I retired to my dad's garage, together with an empty shortbread tin, a drill and some ideas.

I drilled a hole the size of a ten-pence piece in the bottom of the tin. The mic fitted in snugly. Then I drilled holes the size of pinheads in the lid. It was my own invention, although nothing went to the patent office should you fancy making one.

The result? Well, it never made it onto the album, but it was definitely part of the process that led to the final sound.

The song is a repetitive three-chord Spacemen 3 build-up, with a hint of The Who and The Beatles. Lyrically it's about a liaison in the park and is a little short on romance. We weren't taking any drugs to help us write, it was all pure adrenalin, natural energy. Sure, we would go out at night, but the rehearsals were deadly serious. We practised only on Wednesdays and Sundays: Wednesdays from 7 p.m. till midnight, Sundays from 2 till midnight.

So 'Indian Rope', 'Sproston Green' and 'The Only One I Know' were written on a Sunday. I'm not sure whether they have a churchy vibe, but they are heavy on the organ and Rob's dad was a vicar.

It was beautiful, just playing music. I remember coming up with the middle eight for the song 'You Can Talk to Me' on a warm Wednesday evening with Rob, while the rest of the band went to the pub leaving us to get on with it. I would try to hum chord progressions, he would make sense of them on the keyboard. I would dance round the room, shuffling rhythmically, keeping the feeling of constant movement.

A lot of the early song ideas actually came from Martin and Rob. Maybe I would contribute a drum beat or a chorus – and always the lyrics. Martin was the judge; everything had to pass muster with him.

★ ★ ★

From September 1989 till the start of the new decade we were getting big really quickly.

In November, we played the Boardwalk in Manchester,

which held about 300 people. We had to sell tickets ourselves to play, which is often the rule. We must have sold 200 in advance. We had a busload of fifty to sixty kids travelling up from the Midlands, and a rumbling of a following in Manchester. We were opening for Cactus World News, who were popular at the time. But after we played, the place emptied, slashing the audience to fewer than twenty; a sign of the shifting times, maybe?

Our next Boardwalk gig was part of our first UK tour, which kicked off in late January 1990 in support of our debut single, 'Indian Rope'. The gig sold out two weeks in advance.

I gave up my job at ICI in Runcorn in January 1990. As I handed in my resignation, I knew I would never walk through those doors again, but Neil, the boss at the office, kindly said he would keep the position open for me.

I was living at home. I was permanently skint, the curse of those with rock 'n' roll dreams. But somehow I always seemed to be clutching a bag of records and was always on my way to or back from gigs. They were great times.

I would always be working on lyrics, too. 'The Only One I Know' arrived on a late-night walk to the local garage. My Dictaphone went everywhere with me. I was a bit self-conscious about using it, although I was well aware that it had an air of otherworldly cool after I'd seen agent Dale Cooper in *Twin Peaks*.

I always used to channel ideas during my nightly walk and indeed still do. I've been a bit of a pacer all my life, and in those days I would listen intently to instrumental jams on my Walkman while strolling along.

★ ★ ★

We recorded the demo of 'The Only One I Know' in Lanes End Studio, Shropshire.

Steve organized it. He was an important part of what we

were doing. He was older, he had the resources and the fact that he had a record shop meant that, for me at least, we had a cool place to base the best band in the world!

Anyway, before all that we had 'Indian Rope' to record.

I admired the instinctive pop approach of Bernard Sumner and Lou Reed, the unkempt simplicity of Syd Barrett and the disjointed English prole prose of Mark E. Smith. No matter what, you just always seemed to get the real them.

They were my favourite singers, so I did have something to go on. At the same time I have always felt an affinity with guitar players, because maybe I knew deep down I would always have to rely on one. Bowie had Ronson, Mick had Keith; I was looking for whatever it was in Jon Baker. I didn't know then that it wouldn't be him; meanwhile in a rehearsal room somewhere a guitarist called Mark Collins was being the best thing about The Waltones . . .

Recording 'Indian Rope' with Chris Nagle was probably the highlight of my life up to this point. Chris was the engineer for almost all my favourite Factory releases. He was Martin Hannett's sidekick and a producer in his own right. Steve had fixed it all up, and I just thought it was brilliant that we'd be working with him.

We worked the night shift in Strawberry Studios, Stockport, because of the cheaper rates. There was a kitchen which Ian Curtis would have used, a sofa where Paul McCartney must have sat, a bathroom where 10cc would have washed their hair, and a peg on which Bobby Elliott would have hung his hat. The excitement of being in this particular studio was one thing; the thought of ending up with a single from there meant that we had taken another step.

Backing it with a couple of B-sides, we pressed it up on vinyl ourselves, and Steve put it out on his label, which was called Dead Dead Good – a term I used when getting over-excited about anything.

★ ★ ★

We went out on tour in January 1990 to promote the single, and on the first day I had a car crash on the way back from Manchester, outside the Smoker Inn in Knutsford. The woman whose car I hit pulled out suddenly from the central lane into the fast lane. I hit her as I was breaking, but I must have been doing 70 mph, slowing down to about 50 on impact.

A lot of things go through your mind in the seconds before something like this. Would my first record with the band be my last? Had me getting this far just been a cruel joke? Would I be remembered?

I blacked out for a second as the two cars collided with a crunch of metal, followed by the high-pitched screaming of an engine. Then silence.

I opened my eyes, and I was still on the A556, surrounded by smashed glass, a crumpled wing and some gathering rubber-neckers. I ran through a quick physical inventory and, apart from blurred vision, a terrible headache and some whiplash, I seemed to be in working order. I rushed over to the other car to find the driver quite shaken too. She had a broken leg, and she soon left in an ambulance.

My thoughts then turned to that night's gig in Stoke-on-Trent. I ran to the pub and called Steve. He picked me up and dusted me down, and we headed straight for the soundcheck. It turned out that my car was a write-off. I left it where it was and I never saw it again.

★ ★ ★

The tour brought in some great reviews, and the response to the single was incredible. John Robb wrote about us for *Sounds*, and on his recommendation they gave us our first cover feature.

We went to Glasgow, and it now seemed that the further we were from home the more fervent the reaction. We played King

Tut's Wah Wah Hut and Scotland became our home away from home.

I went back to King Tut's many years later, and on the stairs leading up to the live room were the names of some of the bands who'd played their most iconic gigs. 'The Charlatans' was written on the first step.

In Leeds I remember local band The Bridewell Taxis challenging us to some kind of tribal regional punch-up at the Duchess of York. We declined. Present at that Leeds gig was local fanzine writer James Brown. He was one of the first truly inspirational characters that I met on our voyage. At this point the band had been speeding up and down the M1, M6 and A1, word of mouth bringing us most of our new fans. James could see what was happening and knew how to translate the buzz into writing. He had started a fanzine called *Attack On Bzag* in Leeds in the early '80s, and with his fiercely brave writing style, he had taken on the world.

In 1986 he started working at the *NME*, and almost single-handedly altered the face of the paper. At 21, he became their youngest features editor. He was there when it went from selling 70,000 a week to 120,000 a week.

Without taking too long to think about it he documented the times and just went with it. In the excitement and perhaps without them noticing, the old guard were being ushered out. This inspired us. You see someone doing something on a parallel path and it's the affirmation you might not have been looking for – but when you clock it, it inspires and accelerates your work.

Because he was a journalist and I was an artist starting out on my quest, there was a mutual interest that turned into respect, but a kind of distance, too – a reticence about jumping in fully. Perhaps we were both still a little nervous of failure.

If The Stone Roses and The Happy Mondays were first and second in the *NME*'s view of the hierarchy, we were perhaps third, fourth or fifth – but we were James's favourite band. As he moved up the ladder, our trajectory was upwards too, but it wasn't like he was helping us without conviction.

Two things in the *NME* helped power us up: Single of the Week for 'Indian Rope' and a review of our debut London gig at the Powerhouse.

The Charlatans, 'Indian Rope'
(Dead Dead Good)

What really happened when the monkey shot the organ-grinder. A soundtrack for the manic daisy – it is lazy – head, 'Indian Rope' has lashings of eerie organ, trippy vocals and a charisma that'll have the JTQ cowering behind their Hammond and Shaun Ryder trembling in his purple moccasins – the ones he'll only wear inside his flat. Undoubtedly the darlings of top society magazine *Cheshire Life*, The Charlatans stuff you inside their kaleidoscope and fling you back in time to the days when The Doors seemed as dangerous as the Vietnam war and NKOTB were mere pieces of sperm. The groovy 'Indian Rope' is as refreshingly long as it is laid back, an excellent first single.

A Whiter Shade of Male

THE CHARLATANS, LONDON POWERHOUSE

Nine hundred and twenty-four years ago – when William The Conq took Albion – did his victorious forces end each battle with the chant 'Normandy nah nah nah, Normandy nah nah nah'? Just a thought. Tonight the fans, the ones that curve their bodies through that spectacular freakie dancing, are sandwiched between a hard wedge of music industry types bar-side and five boys trading songs from a psychedelic supermarket in front.

Subtlety has been stamped out and layers of excitement and expectation collide eagerly. The difference between the two audiences (fans/industry) is manifold. The spotty beer-bellied bubble heads in their Modernist t-shirts and wide jeans have travelled with the Home-Pride skinned daisy age freaks from Manchester in an international luxury coach. It cost them a tenner for both the ticket to ride and the ticket to enter. The 150 who made the coach, and the hordes who've hit the capital from Aldershot, Cheshire and Wolverhampton, know what they're going to get and they are bristling with anticipation. Theirs is the sound of hyped-up youth and downed lagers.

Leon Trotsky once reckoned that money talks but it don't sing and dance and it don't walk, and the record company men – the managing directors, the A&R people, the agents and the press officers who'd got here in their company cars – proved him right. Gary Crowley joshed with the whole of Phonogram's A&R team; a gaggle of agents predicted how big or small The Charlatans would be in the coming months, the air was thick with corporate but trendy expectation. This is the sound of Big Money smiling.

The Charlatans came on and knocked their teeth out. When bowling ball-eyed singer Tim announced: 'We 're the best band in the world' and sprinted off into a set that attempted whole-heartedly to prove it I was reminded of Peter Hook laying the same claim two years ago. Remembering how poor Revenge were last week, it's clear just how fast things have changed. Splashing away inside a bath of projected oil lamps the five mop-tops played their teenage psycho-delia with passion and confidence. Down the front, amongst the jungle of slack tops and rushing arms, amidst the undisciplined head-rolling and the free-form funk of young bodies, it was a different world to the space by the bar I'd watched the opening numbers from. Stage right, a beefy lad fingered a huge coffin-shaped Hammond organ until it shrieked its hellish harmonies across its followers like some weird entrancing voo-doo hoo-doo. Clear drug music minus the narcissism or drudgery, powered by energy, adoration and mutual excitement. The band weren't so much sexy as brash and naive. Wanting to be cocky but ending up praising the audience. The songs came and went like the colours on a scrambled satellite channel. They opened up with 'Only One I Know' and didn't stop for breath until they were singing 'Sonic' and 'Polar Bear', songs about helicopters and 'looking for the orange ones' – whatever that means. Lining the walls with their merchandising, The Charlatans have got more t-shirts for torsos than they have gigs under the belt; tonight was their 13th. This band infected the capital. It's been difficult for domeheads the last few years, lagging with drug fatigue and retrogressive role models, but The Charlatans manage to give a positive kick to an often old sound. They're exciting and yet shy, but not constipated, irksome, or tight-assed like so many other young bands. Like The Stone Roses they have charisma, it takes a while to stoke itself up but when it starts rolling the energy that bounds between the rhythm section and the Hammond is dynamic. Vocalist Tim lets his vocals ooze gingerly into the crevices and then explodes, his body rattling like the plastic chips in a kaleidoscope.

It isn't their birthplace that's made them interesting, they're not actually from Manchester, nor is it the visual similarities to Ian Brown's brilliant gang, but simply the energy, the throb, the confidence. They've a real feel for what they do. They're Shaun Ryder's children, but this is a whiter shade of male. The times have changed. Here comes the next Vietnam.

According to that week's issue I was Shaun Ryder's younger and prettier brother.

James came backstage after the gig and told us it was the best one he had ever been to. He said he was going to do a big live feature and give us a mention on the cover. We were freaking out. I was worried that it might be too much too soon, but he was convinced we were going to be massive. He stuck to his guns and we were namechecked on the cover like he said.

It gave me a sense of fear, as I'd seen bands hyped who then became whipping boys until they were finished. The inkies, as they were known, the *NME*, *Melody Maker* and *Sounds*, were famous for having a 'we built you up so we'll now knock you down' mentality. Remember Birdland? I didn't want us to become like them – some kind of forgotten footnote. But there was little I could do about it anyway.

I guess that's the similarity between a band and a journalist. James was doing his job and asking us to go along with it, just like we were doing our thing and asking the world to come along with us. Let a dreamer dream.

Dreams can become reality; we were ploughing our own groove, but now we were unwittingly part of a bigger picture. Our generation was making its contribution to music history. Kids were taking lessons learned from punk, and the drug of choice was bringing out a collective euphoria reflected in a blissed-out sound-track. Visually, the fresh, beautiful and debauched photos of Kate Moss by Corinne Day in *The Face* would kick-start heroin chic.

The daisy age was upon us.

It was the first time a band could self-release and get in the Top 75, when *Top of the Pops* was highly relevant and MTV was still mostly a music channel, pre-Facebook, pre-internet, pre-mobile phones. *The Chart Show* was TV's only other Top 40 rundown – no superfluous presenters, just videos. As ever, we watched, and it said we were No. 1 in their indie chart. Then a caption popped up saying that 'Indian Rope' would be featured the following week. Eek! We had no video and no time to make one. Steve didn't know what to do, so he sent them a photo-graph. We were convinced it wouldn't be enough and we'd miss our chance. We still watched anyway, and there it was: on my mum and dad's telly, our song playing to the hungover millions across the UK, alongside the promo shot that Steve had sent them. They had trimmed off the Northwich address.

According to John Robb, writing for *Sounds*, 'the band are the soundtrack to a barmy crew of acid-casual, energy-burning joyheads . . . energy, excitement and execution – the three E's that are counting for so much.' We were being encouraged to help usher in new times. 'Good riddance to the hellfudge zone that was the '80s,' was John's final note in his review from Manchester University in March 1990.

Meanwhile, James Brown was changing the landscape around us, like a single little advance party, causing radio and TV people to sit up and take notice. He filled the gap between the audience and the businessmen, a mad fucker from Leeds into football and Factory Records, stagediving into the middle of it and then mingling with the money men to tell them what they were missing down the front.

★ ★ ★

I remember asking Martin, when we were recording 'Indian Rope', whether he thought we would ever top that song. I just thought it was the best thing I had ever heard.

'Yes, of course we will,' he said, and he was right.

Between 'Indian Rope' and our second single, 'The Only One I Know', I began to trust the people around me, people with experience and enthusiasm like Martin Blunt and James Brown. My natural self-doubt started to melt away.

We had everybody chasing us for a signature: Phonogram, Sire, Island, pretty much all the big guns. But there was one label, Beggars Banquet, that I really liked because they had The Cult, The Fall and Bauhaus. And the rest of the band liked them because they were an independent. Eventually, label boss

Martin Mills got our signature over sandwiches in a pub in Wednesbury, which again we liked. It was a little bit perverse, a million miles away from the Groucho Club.

We liked Martin and his A&R man Roger Trust because they had been turning up at all the gigs no matter what. They drove to a Manchester gig in a blizzard, which was a big deal because the A&R from London Records called up to say he couldn't make it as the weather was too bad.

Beggars went the extra mile, in fact the extra 163 miles, even if it was full of snow. They actually met my mum and dad that night, which was again quite cool. I'm not sure now why it seemed important, but I guess I was still quite young.

Martin promised he could do all a major label could do sales-wise in countries we had never even dreamed of playing, and promised also to give us the freedom we wanted artistically. He said all bands think they have creative and artistic freedom, but if they are signed to a major label, they actually don't. We believed him! We had developed a major-label phobia, and we wanted to be a major act on an indie label. So we signed with Beggars Banquet for a six-album deal, and we went into the studio a couple of weeks later to begin work on our second single and our first for Martin Mills/Beggars Banquet.

We were going to record 'Polar Bear', but when I got to the Windings Studio in Wrexham, Roger Trust had been leaving messages telling us to go with 'The Only One I Know'. We all thought it was a great choice, because the reaction to it at the gigs was off the hook. Steve Harrison, though, didn't agree – he thought it was the wrong way to go. But we went ahead and recorded it, and everything in our lives changed.

'The Only One I Know' is essentially a Northern soul/ Motown record spliced with Iggy Pop's 'Lust for Life' and 'Hush' by Deep Purple, with a Diana Ross intro as the chorus. The lyrics were about being crushed and broken-hearted. We mixed it at Strawberry Studios again, and it became the hit record of the summer of 1990, arguably the biggest world-wide hit of the whole Manchester scene. It was all down to timing. When 'The Only One I Know' broke, the Inspirals were in the charts as well with 'This Is How It Feels to Be Lonely'. Every label seemed to want its own band from that scene, and some monumentally bad bands got signed while others got lost in the crush: The High, Paris Angels, Intastella, World of Twist, The Mock Turtles, Northside, Milltown Brothers, Candyskins, New FADS, The Soup Dragons (even though they were Scottish), Flowered Up (even though they were from London), The Bridewell Taxis (even though they were from Leeds) — you decide what category they belong to.

In May we went on our third tour of 1990, put on by a fledgling Northern promoter called Simon Moran, who had worked with us on our second tour of the year in March. The speed at which things were moving can be seen in the sizes of the venues we were being booked into. In January we played venues of around 80–150 capacity, like Aldershot's Buzz Club, the Wheatsheaf in Stoke and Southampton's Joiners Arms. The March tour was at places like Nottingham Trent Uni, Sheffield Uni and a hometown gig at Manchester Uni, now the Academy 2, with a sold-out crowd of over 900. In June we were playing the Town & Country Club (now the HMV Forum) in London to over 2,300 fans. I was nervous that I was going to be nervous, but, surprisingly, I was freaked out by not being freaked out. It felt really natural and I just went with it. And the more lights we had, the less of the ever-increasing and increasingly enthusiastic audiences I could actually make out.

As we travelled up and down the country in the van, we would turn on the radio and hear our song being played, just like the stars do in those music biog films. No sooner had we picked up a few plays on night-time radio with the likes of John

Peel than we were seemingly A-listed on daytime Radio 1, played six or seven times a day by Simon Bates, 'Ooh' Gary Davies and even Steve Wright. I was imagining kids listening in Dixons, painters and plasterers listening on their scaffolding, our own mums and dads in their kitchens.

In London people would beep their horns, I would look round and strangers would be waving at me. Back home, my mum never had to wait for the bus again, as people were always offering her lifts into Northwich. She was the most recognizable mum in the village.

★ ★ ★

We made our first video with 'The Only One I Know'. Up to then we'd never thought about it – to me videos meant *Thriller*. We made ours in a warehouse near Northwich. There seemed no point in going grand – it would be against the spirit of the band. The only way to do it was get a warehouse, plug in, play loud and let our mates wander in as the word got around.

It was directed by Kim Peters, who designed our first seven singles covers and two album sleeves. He was a graphic-designer pal of Steve Harrison's and was becoming a friend and fan of the band. He was also a bit older than us, and like Steve had been a regular at Eric's in Liverpool.

He was very enthusiastic, but he had never made videos before. We had never made records before, and Steve had never managed anyone before, so it seemed like we were all in it together.

It goes without saying that there was always a posse of people following us, taking drugs and generally hanging out with the band. The video for 'The Only One I Know' was essentially a free warehouse party. And the arrests were real. We filmed the cops taking out a few kids. No one seemed to mind.

Since we were known for our live performances and our accessibility there was no need for a script, a storyline and the usual pop-video flab.

'The Only One I Know' entered the charts at No. 21. 'Indian Rope' had peaked at 89. A single just outside the Top 20 was hard enough to take in, but the following week it broke into the Top 20. The week after that we gathered round the radio to listen to the Top 40 on Radio 1. And we were No. 9. Top 10 singles meant people like David Bowie or even Duran Duran. It was now possible to add our name to that list.

We'd pressed 5,000 copies of 'Indian Rope', which seems like a lot now, but it sold out within a day by word of mouth. We ended up re-pressing and selling 15,000 with just one advert in Sarah Champion's ace Manchester fanzine, *Scam*.

'The Only One I Know' was available in Woolworth's. My nan would see it next to the pic 'n' mix. Some die-hard punks might have called this selling out, but I called it the most exciting time of my life.

The world seemed to be revolving around Manchester. Every magazine, radio station and TV show was overrun with Manc personalities. We went on *The Word*, a TV show hosted by Mancunian motormouth Terry Christian, one of the first people to ever play our music. He had a radio show in Manchester and had played the demo of 'Indian Rope'.

I remember being interviewed on the streets by film crews from London asking what it was like to be a real Mancunian. Of course, I said I was from Salford.

I don't remember hanging out with other bands too much. We were aloof, we were moody, and we kept ourselves to ourselves. We thought that talking to other bands would dilute our spirit or let our secrets out, so we just did our own thing. I'm not sure where these thoughts and attitudes came from, but, remember, we were making it up as we went along. I do, however, recall being quite happy to meet The Pixies. Kim Deal was my favourite bass player and we appeared on *The Word* together.

We went back to the Windings in Wrexham to record our first album. As the 1990 World Cup was starting, 'The Only One I Know' went from No. 9 back to 10, to 15, to 19, and then to 31, where James's 'Come Home', The Inspiral Carpets' 'She Comes in the Fall' and The Soup Dragons' 'I'm Free' were all within five places of us. The record went on to sell over 250,000 copies, and The Charlatans were now public property.

Nationally we had hit a groove, and the next step was to take it international. We started going to radio stations and were asked to do phoners all over the world. It was fun but harder than I ever imagined. Every radio station in America had me recording what they call 'idents', in which I had to claim that I listened to them.

> Hi, this is Tim Burgess from The Charlatans UK, and whenever I'm in town I listen to Mikey Rozenowski's hand-picks on the hour on WMZQ 98.7. Stay tuned for the traffic news at 9.

Just try reading that again out loud without stumbling over any of the words and sounding hugely excited. There are over eighty radio stations in Texas; times that by twenty DJs at each station, times that by fifty states, and you'll see that the task was pretty daunting. But we were keen to go along with it.

Then Radio 1's breakfast presenter Simon Mayo called up, expecting us to jump. I remember answering the phone in the Windings main reception area during the latter stages of the making of our all-consuming debut album. He was giving us Single of the Week for 'The Only One I Know'. He said I had to call in at six in the morning.

Now, the only time I ever saw 6 a.m. in those days was as the end of one day rather than the start of the next. I was still a punk at heart, and chit-chat with breakfast DJs wasn't what

I'd signed up for. I said I couldn't do it because I would be sleeping.

He was furious, the Nicey exterior replaced by the growl of an ogre with a dented ego. He informed me that the one-and-only Billy Joel had called him last week from New York to do his show when he was given Single of the Week. The fact that Billy Joel had done it the previous week encapsulated the very reason I didn't want to.

We turned down a flurry of shows, including *Going Live*, which I liked to watch but which wasn't the type of programme that we thought should figure in our (non-existent) masterplan. We also turned down the Brits because they were organized by Jonathan King.

Further afield, TV appearances were more of a gamble. We were unaware of the content of any given show in, say, Japan, Italy or Spain – but we were slightly less bothered because our mates couldn't see us. Anyway, it was either sit and watch TV in the hotel and not understand it, or actually be on the programme and not understand it. Characters in oversized costumes would often appear, wielding custard pies. In Japan I remember being followed and somewhat upstaged by a Japanese Jimi Hendrix impersonator.

One of the most popular questions I get asked, particularly during UK radio or magazine interviews, is why The Charlatans have lasted so long. To me it's been just as much about what we have turned down as much as what we have done.

So Simon Mayo told me I would never be played on Radio 1 again. Was I claiming to be bigger than Billy Joel? Or Simon Mayo? I was confused. It was like my John Lennon, bigger-than-Jesus moment, except 'Burgess bigger than Mayo' was never going to get quite the same headlines. It felt like we were starting to make enemies already. But, you know, we did get played on Radio 1 again.

This was also the time when I began to tell everyone, tongue firmly in cheek, that we were the most important band in the world. That didn't go down too well either. We were definitely the most important band in the world to me.

The journalists would supply the intoxicants until they got the quote that would appear above the interview or on the cover in bold type. Hotel suite, tea, chips, lager, shots, champagne, disarming nature and sometimes even coke. Almost every inducement would be proffered. Masters of this particular art were the brilliant Stud Brothers from the *Melody Maker*, somewhere between good cop/bad cop and Bert and Ernie.

When our first album, *Some Friendly*, debuted at No. 1, there was a massive editorial in the *Daily Mirror* saying that The Charlatans were the biggest band in the world. Forget Guns N' Roses, forget this, forget that, 'The Charlatans are straight in at No. 1, the first band to achieve this since Johnny Hates Jazz' – OK, I would have preferred someone better, too – almost three years earlier.

If The Stone Roses and The Happy Mondays had opened the door, we invited everyone in and poured the drinks.

We were No. 1. Did I say that?

Ham on rye, hold the mayo.

* * *

Our first ever gig in America was at the Marquee in New York in 1990. It was one of the biggest signs to us that we'd made it, or were at least on our way to making it. We were told that the city's glitterati were there, including Martin Scorsese. I've since learnt that the 14-year-old Mark Ronson was there too, reviewing the gig for a school paper. He'd sneaked out of his mum's house to come and see us.

After a quick trip to Toronto's Horse-Shoe Tavern we then

played the Shoreline Amphitheatre and the Pacific Amphitheatre in San Francisco and Orange County California for Ian Astbury of The Cult. Ian met us off the plane at LAX. He'd invited us to play his festival, called The Gathering of the Tribes. Ian had the idea to really fuck with the genres and bring everyone together – and it worked! The Cult headlined, and he'd asked us as the new buzz band from the UK. There was also Ice-T, Iggy Pop, The Cramps, Public Enemy, Michelle Shocked, Queen Latifah . . . and Joan Baez.

I remember sitting next to Iggy and being about as excited as I'd ever been about sitting near anyone. I was quiet, maybe a bit shy. In fact I didn't say anything at all, and he suddenly jumped up and starts rubbing my head with his knuckles, like some crazed uncle at a wedding, smiling all the time in that manic Iggy (front cover of *Lust for Life*) way. Then he ran off.

We were on early and, because we were rowdy Northerners, were getting quite a lot of attention. We thought we were the bees' knees. We had 40 minutes to do our set but we went over: 42 minutes, 43 minutes, 44 minutes . . . The stage manager was looking at his watch and signalling at us frantically to get off the stage. We were only half way through 'Sproston Green' when he came on and said, 'Dude, you gotta get off!'

As this was going on, I turned round to see Jon Brookes being dragged off his drum stool by some roadie for The Mission, who had earlier made it obvious that they didn't like us by throwing a bottle of Jack Daniels at us on our way on stage. Suddenly this huge commotion broke out. Security were pushing us about, Rob threw a punch, and our manager appeared on the stage. It was all pretty threatening. Until Ice-T stepped in with his crew. They were all wearing bullet-proof vests, which in 1990 meant 'Don't fuck with me', and the message now was, 'Don't fuck with the white guys'.

Ice-T stopped us getting a beating. And, amazingly, we got

asked to play again later in the evening, as an apology. We were told it was because Ice-T had requested it and I'm not going to dispute that. We politely declined.

This was our unofficial invitation into the rock 'n' roll circus, and we took it up with relish.

2. COCAINUS

My love of drugs started early, with smoking – I guess that is a drug. My friends all had older brothers or sisters who smoked. I had my first cigarette when I was 6, nicked from Julie, my best mate Simon Owen's older sister, who was 13. She was smoking Player's No. 6. What could she do? She was unlikely to tell on us, even if she did catch us. I suppose that, growing up in such a small village, I was looking for kicks from very early on because I was really bored. Obviously I didn't smoke all the time at this age, it was just curiosity smoking. I began full time at about 11. At secondary school, by the incinerator, me and my friend David Mills would do a swap: half his sandwiches for half my cigarettes, which I had bought with my dinner money.

I then moved on to solvents: glue/petrol/Gen-Keen, Evo-Stik remover. Lots of my friends had motorbikes, and while they were riding and pulling wheelies, I was doing the less dangerous thing of lying on my face with a plastic bin-liner stuck to my hair. At least it was a cheap way of getting an out-of-body experience. Then, seasonally, there were the magic mushrooms, picked in our own neighbourhood. Growing up in the countryside did have its positives.

I suppose these drugs attracted me because they were free. Although not entirely scot-free: I passed out once in a bin-liner, and when I came round the glue had dried and I had it stuck in my hair; not just a few strands, but all of my hair.

My friends' older brothers were all into acid, so naturally I got into it too – windowpanes and microdots, they were the favourites. Then speed, then hash, but all of this was little more than a passing interest, a buzz and an escape. I loved the fantasy, the thrill aspect of getting high, the way things looked. Everything had a sparkle, a halo and a beauty that would free me from the mundane.

The Haçienda years, especially on Fridays and Saturdays, did this too. They were all about ecstasy. I witnessed the future of music first hand and had some pretty wild sex too, and I'm damned sure that I reached a higher state of consciousness with the help of a pill the size of a mint (they were bigger back then than they are now).

At this point, in the late 1980s, my drug-taking stayed at a constant level of maybe 3.5 or 4 on a scale of 1 to 10 – a couple of pills every weekend and perhaps a couple of spliffs a day, and the odd hit of speed here and there to take the edge off a particularly boring day in Cheshire. Then in the mid '90s I went 10/10, or 11/10. I did coke 24/7. But at that time it felt as though the whole world was at it, 'sprinkling cocaine on their cereals for breakfast', as Noel Gallagher so eloquently put it. It was the moment when coke came out of the bourgeois underground closet and into the hands of the working class. Out of the dark and into the lime-light; or out of the wrap and onto the kitchen table.

I remember getting thrown out of the pub one night for 'three in the toilet': three of us in a stall snorting off the top of the toilet-paper holder. The door wasn't even half shut – we were there for all to see. One of the bar staff came in and told us all to leave. The next morning he got the sack for throwing us out. I was considered 'family' by the owners, who incidentally were both as much into it as I was. We were a nice, cosy, cocaine-snorting family, and they didn't give a fuck what I did.

I was doing a lot of drugs by anybody's reckoning. In the *Evening Standard* I proudly announced I was the New Keith Richards. I was doing more than anyone around me. I did coke quietly and constantly every day pretty much for ten years, and – in my mind, at least – it only had a detrimental effect on my personality during the last two of those ten.

Our tour manager, Neil Mather, told me that I used to steal things all the time when I was on drugs, especially from hotel rooms. Not laptops and wallets or anything like that. I was motivated by swag with much less use or value. Anything shiny though . . . I was a bit of a magpie.

I can be the same with ideas for songs and even lyrics, but only if I need them and love them. I justify it by telling myself that I have paid for music both emotionally and financially all my life, though I appreciate this defence won't stand up in a court of law.

Often as I clanked down some hotel steps with newly ac-quired trinkets in onyx and silver Mather would smile at me, while simultaneously shaking his head. He'd say, 'All right, Timmo? What's that you've got in your pocket? Anything to declare this morning?'

Sometimes if the clanking was especially loud there would be anger mixed with despair: 'Don't you know they'll charge you for that!'

I wasn't so much a thief, more someone who just did all of his shopping in hotel rooms. Think less Ronnie Biggs, more Michael Jackson.

Sometimes the guilt would get the better of me, and Neil would have to return the booty. Or I'd realize I had no use for that pedal bin . . . It looks odd written down, but it all seemed to make sense at the time. Maybe I needed mementos to remind myself about what the fuck I was doing, physical things to tether me to earth. I might not know anything that's going on, but I do have a 6-inch × 4-inch solid-silver platter, a magnifying glass and various backscratchers and shoehorns. I can't recall the last time I bought a towel. The more opulent the hotel, the stronger the feeling of loneliness.

The degrees of oddness and dislocation on a tour can range from simply forgetting your room number to not being able to recall the name of the hotel to being confused about which city you're in. Imagine our bus driver parking up outside the venue, eagerly opening the local Yellow Pages and calling the finest, sexiest local prostitute within his price range of weekly per diems (*per diem* is the Latin phrase for 'daily subsistence money while on tour', roughly, possibly the only Latin regularly spoken by bands and crew). There is a kind of deal about this sort of thing – you don't point out anyone else's weirdness and they'll not point out yours. That leaves a lot of room to let things in. I remember a phase when the band got into a novel way of taking coke. To be precise, we discovered the process of blowing cocaine up each other's arses.

There, I have said it. It's not like we invented the practice, but I realize now it's not an everyday thing for most people.

Drug-use builds in a series of steps that get ever more ridiculous, but they are small, regular steps so it's hard to notice what's happening. They can take you to some bizarre places. If your environment changes slowly and subtly you tend not to notice how nuts everything has got.

We'd heard the tales – possibly apocryphal – of Stevie Nicks engaging in this methodology, and our limited research had pointed out that the rectal nerve endings were much more receptive than their nasal equivalents. My knowledge of this is more hearsay than medical, so if you need any more background information I suggest you look it up.

And let's not talk about this if we ever meet.

Not every member of The Charlatans took part in this highly charged ritual, which has been variously described as having 'a Manhattan powdered doughnut', 'a talcing of Johnson's adult powder' or simply 'a Friday night', for some Hollywood rich kids and stockbroker types.

I was a giver and a receiver. They say giving is better than receiving, but believe me, in this case the giving is not that great but the receiving made it all worthwhile. It was significantly more effective than I had been used to, but then again it would have to be, as the intimacy and proximity needed was much more of a carry on than the more traditional nostril method.

I enjoyed it. As far as I was concerned, it was just another way of getting the drug into my system. When Sunday newspapers expose someone's drug-use, they often headline it as 'My Drug Hell', but as far as I was concerned I was in my drug heaven.

And I was mixing with people who felt the same way. I have never been a snitch, so for purposes of anonymity and dramatization I am going to borrow from *Reservoir Dogs* to describe some partakers.

Mr Pink could no longer take it through his nose after, in his own words, he 'blew it up' in LA on the very first tour he did with us. I was there, I witnessed his massive allergic reaction. He couldn't open his eyes, let alone breathe.

So now he could only *eat* coke: place finger on the line, rub in middle finger, then rub enthusiastically into the gums, if I remember rightly. But then he was the one who devised the technique for our newly discovered practice. It required:

> 1 paper cone – made out of a magazine page or hotel notepaper
> 1 thick straw – ordered on arrival in a round of drinks.
>   Failing that, a $20 bill or a £5 note rolled tightly
> 1 Rizla paper

While you're taking your steady steps to the realms of hedonism, you also become an accidental expert in certain areas. Some of these, like how to minimize the pain of airports and air travel, are necessary for your sanity. Others are just learned through experience and constant use – the cocaine was better if heated, fewer lumps – ground was even better. Did I say I'm not hugely proud of any of this?

The idea was that you sucked the drugs into the straw or banknote, but to ensure you didn't suck them into your own mouth you had a Rizla on the end. It had to be a delicate suck, since you didn't want to get the Rizla wet. You stick the cone pointy-end first into the participant's anus, aim your straw into the cone and blow sharply, like firing a dart from a blowpipe. It has to be precise and well timed. Then wait for it . . . yes! The participant jumps around the room as if someone has rubbed a fiery chilli on the spot.

Richard Pryor famously said, 'Cocaine is God's way of telling you you have too much money.' We were literally and metaphorically shoving our own money up our arses, via other rolled-up money. What was God trying to tell us? Whatever it was, I didn't listen for quite a few years.

★ ★ ★

The paranoia of a drug habit mixed with the claustrophobia and utopian ambience of a tour bus create unconventional situations that are the ideal breeding grounds for eccentric behaviour. If you took five people you worked with and transplanted them to the confines of the back of a tour bus, charging across a continent, from one brightly lit city to another, living like it was New Year's Eve every day and every night, and repeating (to fade) every day for a month, with little more than a pack of cards and a handful of worn DVDs, the whole thing punctuated by irregular stop-offs at the dimly lit mescal-and-grits-laden metropolis of a truck-stop, Little Feat playing in the background, aggressive bikers and prostitutes in the foreground . . . now I am not complaining and I am possibly being defensive, but things would likely get a bit sketchy, wouldn't they?

And this was our life, my life, for sustained lengths of time. On top of this, music does seem to attract the OCD, ADD, bipolar, suicidal, anorexic, bulimic, power-hungry, self-obsessed, self-hating, self-harming and the completely un-self-aware. We were in a travelling cage, a mobile circus. We were a human zoo.

We were always keen to experiment with whatever we could get our hands on, and careful to hold on to whatever we had procured, to keep the monotony at bay: potions, lotions, unguents, powders, pills, poultices, resins and plants. Various acquaintances popping up along the way and wanting to party added to the chaos. They would bring the medicine cabinet, leaving us a little something to help us on our way. One of us was even referred to as the Doctor.

Bearing in mind the sheer amounts we would have in our possession and the fact that border crossings were inevitable, deliveries and intake had to be timed carefully, leading to a rather over-complex stock-control system. We were like a team of monkeys running an Argos shop. Anyone or anything not strapped in could whizz past you at any given time.

Obviously, none of these wares could be put on display. Since bands took to using buses and crossing countries there has been an unofficial game of cat and mouse with those paid to uphold the law. If you get caught, not only do you lose the stash, but tour managers become disgruntled, US visas can become impossible to secure and schedules go into meltdown.

The cops love to humiliate a band. After some bad behaviour on a plane, we were once removed in handcuffs to downtown New York's drunk tank. They took our details slowly and methodically and put us into their clunky conveyor-belt penal system, locking us up, confiscating our belts and shoelaces, and making us listen to their rock 'n' roll stories: 'We had that Axl Rose in here last week.' All so that we would miss our connecting flight to Springfield, of all places. I suppose this was some rite of passage which it would have been more embarrassing to have missed. Stories like this certainly made the time pass quicker in the pubs back in Camden and Manchester.

This happened at the start of our 1995 tour, Hello America. Our opening act were Menswear, and I asked them recently for their memories of the tour:

> Doing a lot of drugs on your tour bus. Speeding from Detroit to Chicago. Going to a David Bowie afterparty in Detroit in some weird industrial club. Playing a great show at that lovely

American Legion Hall. But not a lot of specifics – we were
wasted for a lot of the tour.

Says it all.

★ ★ ★

We always seemed to be accepting delivery of a large amount of
grass on our arrival in Seattle, next stop Vancouver, involving
the most notorious border crossing in the music world. Learning where to stash stuff was key. A tour bus has many a nook
and cranny where illicit small packages can be hidden, though
with the excitement and forgetfulness that all this brings it can
take hours to find them again.

On approaching one border we were eager to make sure we
crossed it with our essentials intact. After hours of staring at the
TV screen, Mr White had noticed that the entire entertainment
system was held in place by a frame secured by a dozen screws.
He thought there would be enough room behind the frame to
accommodate our valuables temporarily, not only the narcotics
themselves but also the paraphernalia: the scales, papers, table-
spoons, baggies, scarred CD cases and Blockbuster cards.

As the bus roared ever closer to the border our team
sprang into action. Mini-screwdrivers were sourced, micro-
engineering was undertaken. Now that Mr Pink was in charge
of the logistics – anything to do with maps and a tool kit – we
knew we were in safe hands. Mr White was almost like an under-
study to Mr Pink, as he had not been around as long.

Mr Blonde was the muscle, the director of movement of anything heavy and breakable. He tried to approach the whole mission
from a scientific point of view. On a tramadol-high through a
broken bone, and mixed with speed, and with a Jack and Coke in
hand, he would be lifting almost twice his bodyweight.

Mr Purple waited quietly for events to unfold, giggling to himself, occasionally mopping a brow, picking up his dropped tools, locating screws lost because of sudden braking or bumps in the road, and chopping out the last couple of lines before the goods were hidden.

Everything was removed, then meticulously replaced. The whole thing was cleaned down by Mr White. Brows were mopped and innocent demeanours faked. I was dispatched to check how far it was to the border.

'Seventeen miles.'

So we were going to be there in twenty minutes?

'No, you idiot, we crossed it seventeen miles ago – they never stopped us.'

Add in the fact that the trip was through the Channel Tunnel. It was dark for much of our operation, but we hadn't noticed. The level of concentration brought about by the very thing we were trying to conceal, mixed with the unique atmosphere of a party bus, made something like this just an everyday occurrence.

* * *

Studios can be disconcerting places, with lots of arrivals and departures – especially when drugs are being ordered and delivered. Odd hours are kept according to the vagaries of creativity. On one occasion I was at the studio in Rockfield, up at the top sleeping quarter in the Coach House. Rob was organizing a coke deal, and there were a lot of frantic phone calls, making arrangements.

It was a Friday night and he was already out of it while trying to resolve the finer details. I can remember how impatient Rob became when the dealer failed to turn up. In his wisdom he decided to go running after another guy in Bristol (the other stuff was supposed to be coming from Newport) and got his roadie, John Clarke, to give him a lift. Cocaine decisions.

Off they went in Rob's orange MG Midget, which he'd restored over a couple of years as a labour of love. I woke at two in the morning in need of some water. I was having a night off everything because I was doing the vocals and had to be as with it as possible. As I opened the door to go out of the bedroom and into the kitchen I noticed a gang of strangers. One of them approached me and asked if I was in The Charlatans. I was still coming round and thought the intruders were perhaps friends with one of the others, but something just didn't seem right. The kid that had walked up to me suddenly pulled a knife and put it to my throat. I was dazed and unsure if it was a dream, but as the adrenalin kicked in, I realized it was definitely real. 'What the fuck is this all about?' I wanted to say, but I was aware that moving my mouth was putting me in closer contact with the blade of his knife. I was talking like a bad ventriloquist, but he must have understood.

He said 'I've got your drugs! And it seems you don't want them now!' I quickly guessed this was the dealer from Newport who'd driven all the way out to Monmouth. Only, Rob and John were in Bristol where Rob was buying someone else's gear. I could understand the dealer's anger. A dealer never wants anyone to back out of a deal, but to leave him with 28 grammes he thought he'd shifted is definitely not advisable. Drug-related misunderstandings always have big repercussions. And against the usual code of the dealer, I'm not sure my adversary hadn't got high on his own supply.

So it was quite a big problem. I was there with a knife at my throat — a knife held by a shaky-handed coke-dealer. His mates were all whooping and shouting, and I was thinking he was quite a big-time dealer who wasn't fucking around. But I got brave and somehow talked him down so the knife was only pointing at my gut. Another bedroom door opened. Martin must have heard the commotion. As everyone turned towards him I made my way to the kitchen!

Eventually we persuaded them to leave, Martin made a cup of tea and Rob returned from his trip to Bristol. Not exactly a regular night, but certainly something we had come to expect in our dysfunctional existence while making a record.

★ ★ ★

Part of the game with being into drugs is scoring them. My day revolved around it, and I could think of nothing else.

Some of my best friends over the years were drug dealers. Two of my favourites were someone we knew as Harry the Dog and another fellah affectionately known as 'Drug Dealer' Dave. With the level of anonymity required for successful narcotics trading, the Drug Dealer bit of his name was a surprise. But then again he was also known in some circles as Daft Dave . . .

Once, I organized a meet-up with Dave at the Coach and Horses, an LA English pub on Sunset Boulevard. As I was walking across the car park, I spotted him. He was always nervous about appearing too conspicuous but this was a man with the words 'drug' and 'dealer' in his name. It was the middle of the summer and he was dressed head to toe as Father Christmas. I think this is what is known as hiding in plain sight. We never got to the bottom of why he was dressed like that but a lot of what Dave did never really came with an explanation.

You won't be surprised to learn that we preferred to use Harry the Dog. Harry got his name because his best friends were dogs. He always owned more than one, even when he had nowhere to live. For a while Harry became our lodger. The lack of common sense involved in offering your drug dealer your couch says a lot about what kind of frame of mind I was in. But also something of the warmth I felt for Harry.

The thing with dealing is that it's a profession that you fall into. A bit like the way you just fall into being a rock 'n' roll star. Neither vocation is recommended by advisors at the job centre, but both lifestyle choices offer interesting, exciting, lucrative though potentially dangerous career paths. An accountant usually sets out to be an accountant, studying hard, passing a series of exams, his heart set on a corner office somewhere in Slough. The drug dealer or rock star is often more defined by a series of failings or setbacks rather than certificates or expense accounts, and this has always made them more attractive in every way to me. Ironically the biggest crook in this story was neither a drug dealer nor a rock star. He was an accountant.

I recently met Howard Marks at a festival I was helping to curate. Although he's no longer a dealer, through his training at Drugs Inc. he has become a legend – a word that gets overused, but Hollywood did turn his story into a film. Using his charm and wit, his personality can light up any room. I'd happily booked him to play at the festival.

Mick Jagger has a different vocation, but he's of a similar age and has been on an equally unique journey. He's also used his personality to get out of scrapes, hang out with royalty and from time to time dance with the devil. He remains someone who can light up a stadium with a shake of his ass and one clap of his hands. If you're born with it and you treat it right it will always be with you. There's just one problem: I don't know what *it* is, precisely. But whatever it is, accountants can definitely tax it, merchandise it and take a percentage. So whether you served your apprenticeship at the Crawdaddy Club, the dreaming spires of Oxford or Terre Haute federal penitentiary, it's your character that determines your path.

The Rolling Stones have been a benchmark since the dawn of British rock 'n' roll in *everything*: gigs, record sales, excess, pain. And always brilliance – from the primitive blues beginnings of

'Hitch Hike' and 'She Said Yeah' through to their dalliance with the Studio 54 New York disco glare of 'Undercover of the Night' and 'Emotional Rescue'. In between there's the late '60s, post-Brian Jones output – the Gram Parsons-influenced, cosmic country-inspired *Beggars Banquet*, *Let It Bleed* and *Sticky Fingers*. Then the Mick Taylor blues, gang-on-the-run, tax-escapees period, with the double whammy of *Exile on Main Street* and *Goats Head Soup*. They were made in France and Jamaica respectively, shaped in the shadow of dark, foreboding and uncertain times. The band never buckled under, whatever was thrown at them.

In 2003, after the release of my solo album *I Believe*, I was asked to open for the Stones at the MEN Arena in Manchester and at London's Wembley Arena. I remember Mick limbering up while I was soundchecking. Given that there was a whole suite of dedicated limbering-up rooms that the lead singer of the main band could have commandeered, I told myself that he just wanted to hear the songs – and I still think that now!

Then The Charlatans opened for The Rolling Stones in 2006 and 2007. I don't know exactly how we came to be the support band of choice, but we knew Ronnie Wood pretty well and Mick had been impressed enough to give me a shout-out at the Manchester gig in front of a very proud Ma and Pa Burgess. Ronnie had played with The Charlatans at Hammersmith Apollo. His daughter Leah and son Jesse were in our support band for the tour, and after a mild case of hustling from me and Mark, we managed not only to get their dad to come along to the gig but we also talked him into strapping on his guitar and joining in for the encores – the classic Faces song 'Stay With Me' and our long-standing closer 'Sproston Green'.

The next time Ronnie came on stage to join us was at the Fleadh Festival in north London, a celebration of Celtic roots music . . . Yeah, me neither! Bob Dylan was headlining that night. Ronnie had played with Dylan in the past, including at the Philadelphia leg of Live Aid. Bob saw him on stage with us at the Fleadh and was keen for them to play together in his head-line slot. Ronnie accepted, though he knew there was no chance of a rehearsal.

The set-list arrived with song titles and keys only. Ronnie, a bundle of excitement and nerves, came scuttling into our dress-ing room with the news. Knowing that I was a huge Dylan fan, he asked me to go through the songs, all fifteen of them, with him. Bob is notorious for keeping people on their toes, famous for not letting anyone know what he is up to from one minute to the next. And Ronnie is quite well known for not being hugely concerned with what is happening from one minute to the next.

He needed gently guiding through the songs he was about to play. Some he had never heard before in his life. I would sing the opening line and he would stare at me, eyes wide, processing the information, as attentive as any person could possibly be. Then as the information shot from brain to fingers, he would respond immediately, launching into a number like he'd been practising it for weeks. I understood what was going on here: all three of us – Bob, Ron and I – are Geminis. Is that relevant? Well, it's my book and I've just said it. It was the Cat chasing the Mouse for the Cheese.

★ ★ ★

'Nobody wants a fat pop star,' is one of Mani from The Stone Roses' favourite lines. I always knew that anyway, but now it was having an impact on my life. At first, doing coke gives you a lithe frame, as the hyperactivity takes hold and minor miracles are seem-ingly achieved with ease. But with sustained use and deeper financial investment the payback arrives: you become bloated and sluggish, and take on the physique of a barrel. A cocky, chatty barrel at that.

My life at this point had reached new levels of madness. I was in my Fat Elvis phase, purely down to immoderate ingestion and greedy on-tour intake. I was wearing bigger sunglasses and eating even bigger sandwiches. I started hating having my picture taken. I was doing way too many drugs and I just didn't feel good. Ever. But being the frontman I felt extra pressure in how I looked and came across.

In every other area of my life I had generally pushed things as far as I could, to see what would happen, and maybe now I wanted to find out what people thought of me with my added pounds. I am happy to admit that previously when I'd seen a great photograph of myself it had made me feel good. But of late I was less enthusiastic, knowing I wasn't at my best. I was way beyond blaming photographers and cameras.

I knew that if I carried on in the direction I was going I would be ushered towards the exit of the rock 'n' roll theme park which I enjoyed so much. Theme parks have signs indicating that you must be over a certain height to go on the rides. The rock 'n' roll theme park has signs saying you must be under a certain size. It's true that a few fatties get through once in a while to comply with EU quotas. But it just didn't suit me. It didn't fit with my vision of myself, or how I imagined people perceived me. Again, I just didn't feel good.

Ironically the world that has a reputation for being the most undisciplined – rock 'n' roll – has areas where in fact it is the most disciplined. I heard that The Rolling Stones eat only once every two days in order to keep the looks that got them to where they are. Even Bill Wyman, who left the band years ago, apparently sticks to this regime.

I was pleased when Ronnie said I reminded him of Jim Morrison. It was flattering, although the lizard king was a long time gone at my age, which was then 37 – so were Sid Vicious, Kurt Cobain, Brian Jones and Ian Curtis. They looked great on every single picture, but of course they were dead before the years took their toll.

The truth was, I didn't have a template by which to live my life any more. General wear and tear was having its way with me. Even Ronnie Wood noticed.

3. ARMED ROBBERY

Then came 'Then' – our third release before the album. We had another Top 20 hit. It came out in September 1990 and reached No. 12 in the UK singles chart. A month later, on 8 October, our debut album, *Some Friendly*, was released. Have you got *Some Friendly*? Put it on, make yourself comfortable. Let's go through it together.

1. 'You're Not Very Well'

Lyrically this is a personal view, a social-commentary snapshot. Images of return visits to a now less familiar home, reflections on meandering round a Manchester I was now steadily drifting away from, feeling like an outsider.

The song was originally called 'Some Friendly' – we switched the name for the sake of having a killer LP title. Musically, it was worked out live in front of an audience around Martin's funk bass line and the melody refrain 'You're not very well are you?', with a signature Jon Baker lead-guitar solo.

The title is a tough love letter to city life, with the song breaking down in the middle and becoming more personal. It was the first track on the album, and I was aiming for a clarion call to the disenfranchised. It was also the sound of a big fish leaving a small pond.

2. 'White Shirt'

Musically, this is inspired by Felt, a band who, I would go so far as to say, are the best thing to come out of Birmingham. If you need proof, check out the singles 'Ballad of the Band' and 'Primitive Painters' or the albums *Poem of the River* and *Me and a Monkey on the Moon*. Arguably, on any other day you could give that accolade to Swell Maps! Though if I was doing a DJ set right now I would quite happily slot 'White Shirt' in with 'Me and the Major'/'The Boy with the Arab Strap' by Belle and Sebastian and 'Twisterella' by Ride.

When we were writing this song, I remember thinking about The Brilliant Corners' 'What's in a Word', Medway band The

Claim's 1985 album *Armstrong's Revenge and Other Short Stories*, and Primal Scream's *Sonic Flower Groove*.

Other people just said The Stone Roses. Ah, well.

This song is about clubs and their draconian dress codes, the eponymous attire representing bland but necessary conformity enabling someone to go out at the weekend. It was a paean, an aching for a minor revolution, and once those small statues had been knocked over it would open up more possibilities. Now everyone wears a Ramones t-shirt.

I saw myself as 'a stain on society's white shirt'. That was fine by me, as I was a punk.

3. 'The Only One I Know'

Surprisingly, perhaps, we wanted to omit this track from the finished album. We were going for a Jam, Clash, Beatles or Joy Division 'big song not included' statement. As a compromise, our label, Beggars Banquet, asked us if we would consider including it on the CD version. We agreed, as we gave less credence to that format, though around that time it was actually the way most people were beginning to buy their music.

Lyrically, it's about being a broken-hearted young man, still hoping to find true love. I borrowed the title from 'You're Not the Only One I Know', by The Sundays – a band I was listening to a lot at the time, on my way to rehearsals. Have you got *Reading, Writing and Arithmetic*? Stick it on. (This must be making a mess of your CDs.) The album title is actually a reference to their hometown in Berkshire rather than the thing you're doing with this book right now.

'The Only One I Know' has become a classic – Rob Collins said he got lighter treatment in prison because of this song. He walked into the bathroom nervously on arrival, with thoughts of that scene from *Scum* at the forefront of his mind. A heavy-set guy followed him in – and broke into the opening verse and told Rob that he was a big fan of the band.

It's the song that started it all. We gave it a new lease of life recently with a re-recording we did at the request of David Lynch, for his foundation for education via transcendental meditation. It's the gift that keeps on giving, as the chance to work with such a legendary figure was a high point for me.

4. 'Opportunity'

This time the title is adapted from a Pet Shop Boys single, 'Opportunities', though it was originally entitled 'Love Senses Chaos'.

The first part of the song is a stream-of-consciousness state-ment, written mostly in London and about being in love. It was inspired, though, by the poll tax riots in London in 1990 when I walked out of Goodge Street tube station to see absolute carn-age on the streets – smashed shop windows, cars and buses on fire. It was like a war zone.

Midway through, the song appears to refer to me hating my own body, which I did at the time, but, then again, who doesn't? Maybe it wasn't deep-rooted at all, maybe it was just because I only managed to throw a brick in the riots. It felt good but I was hugely disappointed in myself afterwards, thinking, what I am doing with the band is actually more positive than throw-ing a brick at a policeman. Maybe I was just acting out my Jimmy from *Quadrophenia* fantasy.

Musically, the song was inspired by Talk Talk's 'Life's What You Make It'. We boiled down their optimistic title into one word.

5. 'Then'

Four tracks in and the album has its groove. This song, our third single, starts with the line 'I wanna bomb your submarine'. I was writing it at the time of rumblings of war in the Gulf – I was trying to imagine a relentless pursuit, something unstoppable. I'm not sure whether I got it, but that's one of my favourite lines to sing.

The vocals are dreamy, about losing yourself – your direction or your edge. It's psychedelic garage, with a trace of The Cocteau Twins' shimmer. One of the music weeklies described 'Then' as us going all Emerson, Lake & Palmer, a nod to Rob's sublime take-no-prisoners Hammond solo.

6. '109 Part 2'

Track 6 and things take a turn for the experimental – no singing for starters. I always loved the fact that *Pet Sounds* had a couple of instrumentals.

Essentially it's a remix/reworking of the B-side to 'The Only One I Know', hence the Part 2 bit. The rest of the title is taken from a type of flying boat that I'd seen on the cover of a novel of the same name. I never got past the cover.

It's not strictly an instrumental, as it features the voice of Robert De Niro. But more about that later!

<<<<<<<<<<<<*Coffee break*>>>>>>>>>>

7. 'Polar Bear'

This was originally entitled 'Looking for the Orange One', but again we decided to keep the name for something else. This time it was for our fanzine.

The song features the lyric 'Life's a bag of Revels – I am looking for the orange one' – thus pre-dating Forrest Gump's filmic linking of life and confectionery by about four years.

Andy Bell from Oasis/Hurricane Number 1/Ride/Beady Eye said that he read that we had a song called 'Polar Bear' and liked the title so much that he used it for one of his songs on Ride's debut LP. The cheek of it! I was amused and flattered, but even if I hadn't been, what could I say after all my liberal poaching?

The outro leans towards The Beatles' 'Hey Bulldog', and I think I just heard a bit of 'Breathe' by The Prodigy in there.

This was the album's dancefloor track. I've heard it a few times in clubs, and I think it works pretty well.

8. 'Believe You Me'

This is a Rob Collins gem – a one-man show splicing Jimi Hendrix's 'Crosstown Traffic' with The Spencer Davis Group's 'Gimme Some Lovin'', alongside 5th Dimension's 'Age of Aquarius' and a touch of Booker T's 'Soul Limbo'. I felt it didn't need a whole lot more from me.

Lyrically and emotionally it references 'Ultraviolence' by New Order. I wanted to get that kind of animosity into the song.

Up until our 2011 twentieth-anniversary gigs, this one had slipped down the back of the sofa – from some time in 1991. It was great to rediscover it and play it at the four shows at

London's Roundhouse, Glasgow's Barrowlands, Blackpool's Empress Ballroom and at Primavera Sound in Barcelona.

9. 'Flower'

This is my favourite song on the album. About saying goodbye to a cold and hollow relationship, it was musically inspired by The Pixies and by Rain Parade's 'This Can't Be Today'.

I sang the vocal in the garden at the Windings Studio with Rob Collins throwing stones at me just to get a reaction. It has a great organ and bass sound which reminds me of Nirvana's 'Come As You Are'.

It was the first song we wrote together and collectively said, 'Wow! We really are the best band around.' It was this song that flagged what we were to become.

10. 'Sonic (Think About It)'

The Doors' 'Riders on the Storm' mixed with Johnny Leyton's 'Johnny Remember Me', resulting in a '50s-inspired Madchester song, anyone? I'd been listening in the car to the Joe Meek's Girls' LP and It's Immaterial.

The vocals are very innocent. I had two ideas: one was about living in a painting, and as the painting comes alive so do I; the second was about a girl who disintegrates through drugs and needs my help. For some reason I used always to think people needed my help.

The title came from Spacemen 3's 'Sonic Boom', Primal Scream's LP *Sonic Flower Groove* and even garage favourites The Sonics. Josh from The Horrors told me it was his favourite song of ours.

It's our first and last song with a drum solo.

11. 'Sproston Green'

Sproston Green is a place just off the M6, close to Middlewich – a small field, unknown to many but meaning different things to all who live near by. Like countless similar places around the globe it has an otherworldliness to it. It's a stop-off point for dreaming, romantic liaisons, scraps, naps and general kick-abouts.

I would never have imagined that we would end all of our shows apart from a handful with this song (we weren't sure if a Rolling Stones audience would lap up a non-single that would have eaten up a third of our set time, so for those gigs we dropped it). However, for the ones who have loved us longest and lost their minds and shoes to us the most, this song is the signal to let you know you can go crazy one last time before going home.

It was remixed by super-producer and U2 stalwart Flood for a US single to follow up the success of 'The Only One I Know', with an accompanying Kim Peters video filmed at the Manchester Apollo. The Americans saw this song as the most suitable follow-up.

The proposed UK follow-up to 'Sproston Green' was 'White Shirt', video to be directed by Julien Temple, who had directed *Absolute Beginners* and *The Great Rock 'n' Roll Swindle*. Phone calls were made, plans were hatched, but we were eager to move on and leave the world of *Some Friendly* behind and get started on the follow-up.

We were even offered a six-week tour of America with former Bauhaus singer Peter Murphy, but we were too frazzled. I don't know how much fun it would have been at that time, in front of someone else's audience, feeling the way we felt, though we didn't dismiss it out of hand. Maybe I had just got accustomed to being the centre of attention. We politely declined.

Musically 'Sproston Green' had the engine of Steppenwolf's 'Born to be Wild', the monumental layers of Spacemen 3, and the atmospheric drama of 'Won't Get Fooled Again' by The Who. And a finale containing the rumble of a departing Tardis on its way to another dimension.

The song became so popular that the council eventually stopped replacing the signs at Sproston Green after they were endlessly stolen by our overeager fans. One of the giant signs emerged out of the crowd at a Glasgow gig, only to get swallowed up and disappear again.

★ ★ ★

Some Friendly went to No. 1.

Back in the rehearsal room in Wednesbury, the songs just kept on coming. By our reckoning we would have a new album good to go within a few months, but our record company wanted us to lift one more song from *Some Friendly*. That suggestion hit a brick wall. A compromise was agreed upon when it was suggested that three new tracks would form an EP alongside a remix of 'Opportunity' from *Some Friendly*. It became 'Opportunity Three'.

We already had four songs finished and ready to record, one too many for the EP: 'Happen to Die', 'Can't Even Be Bothered', 'Over Rising (Are You Real)' and 'Way Up There'. After much discussion it was agreed that 'Can't Even Be Bothered' was the ideal springboard for the next album.

Once we'd recorded the EP, the Gulf War stuck its nose into our business. In the same way that Massive Attack had the second half of their name removed by censors and The KLF lost the machine gun intro to '3 a.m. Eternal', we were told that 'Happen to Die' was unsuitable for radio play as long as the war continued. From the two remaining tracks we chose 'Over Rising' as the lead. We got the total time of all four tracks down to just under 20 minutes by way of a last-minute harsh fade-out on 'Happen to Die', so it could count as an EP and not an album, and after its release on 25 February 1991 it rose to No. 15 in the charts.

We'd started off so well that in some ways people were viewing this as a kind of dip in fortune. It wasn't like that for us: we were still on a high from the album being such a success, especially since some people had doubted that we could even get it together to write a whole LP in the first place.

Our follow-up album, *Between 10th and 11th*, was named after the location of the venue of our debut US show. It entered the UK charts at 21, but it spawned our biggest single in America, 'Weirdo', which topped their 'modern rock' chart.

By now the Madchester scene was fading, and some critics dismissed our new album as a failure when compared to the massive success of *Some Friendly*. We'd decided *Between 10th and 11th* would be more experimental and electronic. We were told we could work with anyone we wanted. We met REM's producer Scott Litt after our Royal Albert Hall gig in June 1991. He was a real possibility. We were all REM fans, and I guess we were a worldwide band now.

Other producers had their credentials thrown into the ring, too, lists of albums and triumphs by an array of names. One of those suggested was Flood. He had been the assistant engineer on New Order's *Movement* and was coming off the back of huge success producing both U2's *Joshua Tree* and *Violator* by Depeche Mode. Plus we liked him and knew how he worked after he'd remixed 'Sproston Green' and 'Opportunity'.

His was the name we all agreed on. We didn't realize it at the time, but The Charlatans really needed him. It turned out to be such a great experience. He really moved us forward as a band.

The only thing was, at that point we didn't have enough songs, following the release of the album *Some Friendly* and the subsequent EPs *Over Rising* and *Me. In Time*. It felt right to have so much material being released, but when we came to record *Between 10th and 11th* we had only two new songs written and ready: 'Can't Even Be Bothered' and 'Weirdo'. We were keen on making and releasing new and fresh sounds. I suppose we were naive – or perhaps just uncynical.

We were fans of The Clash, and they had done plenty of singles that didn't appear on albums. But the practice seemed to be dying out, songs were getting referred to as 'product' and bands were having less and less say, as investment in them by the major labels had to be recouped. We, though, were reaping the benefits of being on an indie label, and anyway we'd proved ourselves. As a result we were able to do as we pleased.

In the end, we wrote most of the second album in the studio complex at Rockfield in the Quadrangle, pens, paper and instruments in my bedroom. Everything else was done in the TV room.

After a run of gigs that included the Free Trade Hall, Manchester, the Royal Albert Hall and the one-time biggest festival in the world, Roskilde, where we played directly after The Allman Brothers, we realized we had a problem. Without putting too fine a point on it, Jon Baker's guitar-playing just wasn't up to scratch. We were a band, a gang, and we'd done this together, but, as the saying goes, you're only as strong as your weakest link. And it was increasingly apparent that our first sign of weakness was Jon. We'd gone from rehearsing in Wednesbury to playing sell-out shows across America, and people now began to rely on us.

We were only as sensitive to each other's feelings and emotions as people in their early 20s can be, i.e. not very. We told the world's press that Jon Baker had left of his own accord because things had got too much for him. He'd decided that he wanted to play in more underground bands. Martin occasionally chipped in with the Syd Barrett and Peter Green excuse that Jon had taken up gardening.

The truth? Well, it was a foggy mixture of lots of the above, but whatever the reason, Jon's head just seemed to be somewhere else. And the band demanded full concentration and 100 per cent commitment.

I had become friends with Jon and felt terrible about the looming showdown. But, being the last to join, I felt it best not to say too much. Or maybe I was just chickening out. Anyway, however we tried to dress it up, whichever way we looked at it, Jon's time was up. The cracks had started to show just after the debut album, when there would be not so subtle hints like, 'Hey, Jon, you should go and get guitar lessons.' I'd been for a few singing lessons, because I wanted to push myself, but Jon was treading water.

By early 1991, when we were recording the *Over Rising* EP, the banter had become taunts and the taunts were mutating into what some people might construe as bullying. This is not something I am proud of, but we were in deep, and, like Hunter S. Thompson said, 'When the going gets weird – the weird turn pro.'

We came home after playing the Belfort festival in France, and were back under the microscope of the rehearsal room. Jon Brookes and myself were sent home early while Martin and Rob talked to Jon Baker. I think he knew it was coming, though he later told his friends and family that it was the hardest time of his life. It may not have seemed it, but it was really hard for us as well.

There was no back-up plan. However, we had all been writing and felt confident that anyone we asked would want to join us. No advert was placed, but try-outs were arranged, and first up was a guitarist from a band called The Honey Turtles. They had supported us on some dates and they had a similar sound.

Their song 'Don't You Know' got played on Mark Goodier's Radio 1 show.

He sounded great on the tape he had sent in and he was a great guy. Martin really wanted him in, but there was something that was niggling me. We went out for a smoke and I found out that something was worrying Rob, too.

'He's tiny, mate!' he said. Which is exactly what I was thinking. My thoughts had turned to photographs, vain as this may seem. At 5 feet 10 I was by no means the tallest in the band, but I reckoned that if he joined then photographers would struggle to fit us all in, top to bottom. In my eyes the look of the band was right up there with the sound.

So he got three No's and one Yes. Our search would go on.

The guitarist in The Waltones had caught my eye. I had seen them play at the Boardwalk and the Haçienda, and he stood out. I heard he was now playing with ex-members of The Bodines in a new band called Medalark 11, who were signed to Creation, and that he was also doing merchandise and driving for The Inspiral Carpets. We got a message to him, and some time in July '91 Mark Collins (no relation to Rob, incidentally) turned up with a view to joining The Charlatans. When he walked through the door at Rich Bitch Rehearsal Rooms in Selly Oak, Birmingham, he apparently thought we were only after a second guitarist.

Ladies and gentlemen, I give you The Charlatans Mk 4. This would be the last line-up change we would make out of choice.

Mark and I became inseparable. He was the Keith to my Mick that I had been looking for. He was into The Beatles, The Byrds and The Smiths, his guitar-playing had a natural chime, and he possessed a swagger and bags of the right kind of attitude. He was another Mancunian and we spoke the same language – in a similar accent.

History tells us that breaking up an original line-up in public can have catastrophic results, but Mark's arrival brought a new-found stability which meant we could look much further into the future.

The opening chords of *Between 10th and 11th* put Mark slap bang at the front. It shows how keen he was to pick up the gauntlet.

* * *

When we handed the album in to the label it was called *Anti-clockwise*, and some of the early promos went out under that name. But it got a last-minute change when we decided that *Anticlockwise* was too negative.

I had found myself a new spiritual home in New York City and had met some new friends there. I'd decided that I would split my time for a while between the East Village in New York, Chiswick in London, and my mum and dad's place in Moulton. So I also felt a reference to New York would be more positive than the backwards-spinning sound of *Anticlockwise*.

The cover was a homage to Andy Warhol. I'd bought a rare copy of the Velvet Underground and Nico LP for $200 in Bleecker Bob's Records on 118 West 3rd Street. I blew a week's per diems on it. It was expensive because it was one of the first pressings, with the picture of Emerson on the back of the sleeve and with the peelable banana. Emerson was an 'it' boy, an 'acid-freak' and a member of the band The Magic Tramps. He'd threatened a lawsuit unless he got paid for the use of his image – they withdrew the sleeve rather than agree, but some had sneaked out and one was now mine.

The inside sleeve of our album had the lyrics and various headshots of the band taken by *NME/Select* photographer Steve Double. While the rest of the band have a moody coolness, myself and Jon Brookes are sporting rather serious black eyes. The honest truth is that I can't remember how they got there,

although it's not beyond the realms of possibility that his was done by me and mine was done by him.

Jon and I are perhaps the most volatile members of the band, and from time to time blows have been exchanged, either in the privacy of the rehearsal room or the more public arena of a soundcheck, sometimes over a bum note, sometimes over a sandwich. Like siblings in a dysfunctional family it's never got in the way of our love for each other, but, as in all families, it's not always pretty.

I was consumed by NYC. Like any music fan I pictured John Lennon arriving from a '60s Liverpool, Lou Reed and Laurie Anderson in Central Park, and The Ramones goofing around in the Bowery. I hoped I would bump into Debbie Harry. I stood outside the Silk Building in NoHo where both Keith Richards and Cher owned entire floors. Influenced by all this, our song titles started to take a dark turn and our electronic influences surfaced.

'Can't Even Be Bothered' was the natural follow-up to *Some Friendly*'s 'Flower'. '(No one) not even the rain' referenced e e cummings via Woody Allen's *Hannah and Her Sisters*. It ends with a tribute to Throbbing Gristle's *20 Jazz Funk Greats* as the outro. 'Chewing Gum Weekend' was a less than subtle post-party comedown tale.

For the sessions Rob bought an Emulator sampler that he never used, at least never as an Emulator. To him it was a shelf for coats, ashtrays and precariously balanced cups of tea. In the studio he spent much of his time playing darts and table tennis – while coming up with the amazing melodies, riffs and harmonies of 'Tremelo Song', 'Weirdo' and 'The End of Everything' between his games.

As well as playing keyboards, Rob sang backing vocals. Singing harmonies live with Rob gave me one of the best feelings. Sometimes the only thing we had to go on was a look in the eye, since we couldn't hear each other most of the time, but a glance would keep us in tune. It's a very intimate and sometimes uncomfortable sensation, but when we sang together it was incredibly soulful and one of the most personal and satisfying feelings I have ever experienced. I always thought Rob was a better singer than me. Not only wasn't I the best singer in the world, I wasn't even the best singer in The Charlatans.

Mark brought in lots of pedals and guitar effects, and alongside them he brought amazing quality – like George Harrison, Johnny Marr or a *Forever Changes*-era Arthur Lee. He fitted in perfectly and had a competitive spirit that drove him, and in turn us, forwards – we learned to play chess, which he soon mastered, and he always beat me. I could see how he'd become such a great guitarist and he made it look effortless.

I loved The Byrds, Mark loved The Byrds, The Byrds did Dylan the best and took his songs to the top of the charts. I started studying Bob Dylan at this time, at first casually then discovering all the layers in his work. I was enthusing over *Bringing It All Back Home*, *Highway 61 Revisited* and *Blonde on Blonde*. Anyone wanting a beginner's guide to Bob should start here. I hoped traces of Dylan would seep into my writing.

But in truth I was finding songwriting more difficult. Martin had become critical of my lyrics, to the extent that I could hardly write any more. I felt I was losing whatever it was that had come naturally to me in the beginning.

Martin was actually in a bad way. He had taken our domestic dip in success the hardest. He became increasingly distant towards all of us, and communication dried up. He seemed to be inching closer to the edge. Things came to a head in an apparently trivial incident, when he went to the supermarket for some dog food and mistakenly returned with cat food. It seemed to trigger a kind of breakdown.

He needed some time off, so we decided to cut our touring short and come home. Touring and studio life can take its toll on anyone. It's a terrible cocktail of erratic air-conditioning, muddled time zones and languages, grip-and-grins with excitable marketing executives, introductions to label associates from across the globe, baggage reclaim and resultant lost luggage, airports, radio stations, hotel lobbies and dressing rooms. Imagine all of this shaken with Jack Daniels and served on the rocks to a jet-lagged band, crew, roadies, truck drivers, bus drivers and groupies – who are most of the time either on drugs or desperate to find them. It's difficult after a few days, impossible after a week, becoming near fatal after a month.

Don't get me wrong – the good times are amazing. But the bits in between can be extremely damaging. It's either nothing happening for seven hours, or an intense need to get things done. From the joy of thousands of fans packed into a venue to the loneliness of nobody to talk to at a hotel full of businessmen.

This lifestyle has claimed a near endless list of casualties over the last fifty years. Throw in the almost inevitable self-doubt, an addictive nature or a need to impress, and you are in for a major storm in your teacup. When your confidence is knocked, you pay more attention to the reaction elicited by something than to your own view of it. You become a slave to other people's opinions.

★ ★ ★

After the electronic sounds and the attempted far-outyness of *Between 10th and 11th*, we decided the third LP would be a stripped-down, back-to-basics affair. We were rehearsing in Heaton Norris, Stockport, at the Greenhouse, enjoying recording new ideas on our little 4-track cassette recorder.

In some ways, I feel *Up to Our Hips* was our first serious album. 'Can't Get Out of Bed' – everyone seemed to think it was our finest song to date – would be the first single from it. But 'Jesus

Hairdo', 'Inside-Looking Out' and 'I Never Want an Easy Life' were all highlights. Mark and I had written 'Another Rider Up In Flames' just by ourselves, out of necessity really, as this was the album where we had to write everything quickly.

We were about to enter an unexpected, forced sabbatical. The band were all dedicated fans of the rock 'n' roll lifestyle, and we had picked up quite a reputation for enjoying a party. Rob in particular had taken to it like a duck to water. He had always enjoyed living for the moment. In fact it was something people really admired in him. He had a natural cool that attracted and intrigued people. One of the characters who really looked up to him was a guy who went by the name of Michael 'Ratty' Whitehouse.

We had just got back from a tour of Japan. Rob was a fully paid-up rock star now, and I'm sure his mates thought that his globetrotting meant they would have to raise the bar on their antics in order to impress him. We would often find out about his escapades the following morning and help pick up the pieces of whatever had gone wrong. But on this particular day it seemed much more serious.

I'd been at my mum and dad's at Moulton and was waiting for Martin to collect me for a practice. Steve Harrison called and informed me there would be no rehearsal as Rob was being held in the cells at Cannock Police Station.

This wasn't hugely surprising, considering Rob's past scrapes. I was sure that there was some kind of mix-up, though, when we were told that he was under arrest for his part in an armed robbery. Armed robbery just sounded so *serious*. A lot of bands would have members caught up in drug misdemeanours, hotel trashings, and various bust-ups, but definitely not an armed robbery.

It transpired that no armed robbery had actually taken place, though Ratty was definitely armed. The word 'bungled' was now being used. That made it sound funny, but Rob was only just married and had a young daughter, which turned the whole thing into a disaster.

Details were initially thin on the ground, but as more news came out we put the information together like a jigsaw. For years it would puzzle people how Rob had managed to involve himself in something so serious – the band was doing well, we had a future.

Later, Rob was to tell me his side of the story. He had invested some of his share of our early financial success in a rather smart bright red BMW. He loved the idea that people could see how well he was doing. We were all proud of what we had achieved, and we'd become local celebrities. There was always a big guest list at the gigs and a revolving door of hangers-on and associates. On the day in question Rob had seen Ratty and pulled over to offer him a lift. Ratty was always one to rise to a dodgy challenge, and he was always out to impress Rob. As they passed an off-licence in Cannock, Ratty exclaimed, 'I could do that place over if I wanted.' Rob came back with something sarcastic, thinking Ratty's bravado was getting the better of him. He then pulled on the handbrake and called his bluff. It was at this point that things escalated, as Ratty pulled out an imitation pistol; an imitation, but realistic enough to scare anyone looking down its barrel.

Rob was still sure it was all a show of machismo. 'Go and get me some chewing gum, then,' or some such put-down was Rob's retort. Whatever the details of what went on in the shop, 'bungled' does seem to capture it. Ratty pulled out the gun but the shopkeeper was no pushover. He produced a customized baseball bat from behind the counter. The nails sticking out of it were enough to make Ratty turn tail and run. The bat-wielding shopowner was in hot pursuit. They actually ran past Rob's car, from where he was watching events unfold, smoking a cigarette and listening to the radio. The chase was abandoned, but Rob, still unaware of what exactly had taken place, picked up his passenger – while the police were being called and given the registration number of his car. Still not sensing the seriousness of what had taken place, Rob drove to a pub in Wednesbury to call in on Jon Brookes. Soon, Ratty was bragging about his exploits. Apparently, he was pretending to shoot the gun when they drove out of the car park, making a noise, shooting fake bullets or whatever it is you do when you've just bungled an armed robbery.

When he arrived home, Rob was met by armed police on his garage roof, and his wife and daughter were under armed guard in the house – the police were unsure who exactly was involved. As he pulled up, undercover officers leapt from their cars and handcuffed him after getting him to lie face down on the pavement. He'd really done it this time. Steve Harrison and the band's lawyer, Stephen Lea, were called, and we were all informed.

The original charges were attempted robbery and possession of a firearm, which could result in five years in prison. But Rob's solicitor and Stephen Lea managed to get the charges adjusted to assisting an offender after a crime. The idea then was to convince the judge that, seeing as Rob had had a No. 1 album, he was hardly likely to do over an off-licence for a hundred quid. Added to that, he was using his own car.

Rob was held in the cells and didn't say anything for two days. Then he was told that Whitehouse had owned up to it all, so on the third day Rob told them everything.

Harrison and Lea came up with a game plan to get Rob bail. Once he was out, my not-very-helpful suggestion was for him to do a runner, but apparently he had had to surrender his passport – and it was pointed out to him (and to me) that to abscond while being in a high-profile band might be difficult.

At the end of the trial Ratty was sentenced first, and the judge read it out really slowly: 'Michael Whitehouse, you are sentenced to . . . four . . . years.'

Everybody gasped. Then the judge came to Rob: 'Robert

James Collins, you are sentenced to eight [Rob just thought, 'Oh, shit'] . . . months. Take them down.'

Rob's temporary new home, Her Majesty's Prison Shrewsbury, or the Dana as it was known, was a hangover from the Victorian age. It was severely overcrowded at the time, and still is, and it is currently earmarked for closure. Suicides were rife: there were three in one particularly grim fortnight. Being Victorian meant that not only was it crumbling and antiquated, but it had also been the site of multiple hangings sanctioned by the state.

Our thoughts of it being like the 1970s TV series *Porridge* were quickly dispelled. During visits, Rob's wife and family would be searched and herded through gates and metal detectors, to see him in a prison uniform and high-viz tabard.

On the plus side Rob's status inside was just about as high as it could be – he had been found guilty of involvement in an armed robbery and he was in a band that was in the charts. There isn't much glamour in prison, but with that background and his affable nature Rob was an instant hit.

Unfortunately, in prisons even the plus sides have their problems. The rules of the outside world don't apply, and the further up the prison food chain these people were, the more bad news they would be. It's no surprise that prison warders are out for a quiet life and they generally don't get in the way of anything that will keep their captives subdued. Rob spoke of the availability of every drug imaginable, and we were hoping he had resisted.

The judge had appeared to be letting him off lightly when he passed sentence, but what happened in those few months had a marked effect on him. Prison did change him, but it certainly wasn't for the better.

In some ways this was the beginning of the end for Rob. He was hardly a criminal, but he would never get his life together properly again. He withdrew into himself and had an ever-growing fan club of ex-cons and junkies following his every move. He seemed more and more aloof. He was into much harder drugs now, his eyes pretty much permanently glazed. Flashes of the old Rob would come back, but his fire, if not completely out, had faded in the time he was away.

For the last part of his sentence Rob was moved to an open prison, but that was not as easy as it sounds – people move about a lot more freely in an open prison, but there are cliques and pecking orders, and Rob found it just as tough. Workers in the gardens would arrange with family and friends to bury bottles of spirits, which an eager Rob would then dig up, dust down and be the toast of the wing.

On the scheduled day of his release, 3 February 1994, the prison received a call from Rob's brother enquiring what time he would be coming out, as he was planning to collect him. The only thing was, Rob didn't have a brother. The prison officers figured it was a sleazy journalist looking for a story, so he was released without fanfare through the back door half an hour early. I don't know where most prisoners go when they get out, but, as ever, Rob Collins lived by a different set of rules. A car collected him and we were reunited at the *Top of the Pops* studio for our performance of our new single, 'Can't Get Out of Bed'. (The B-side of the single, sweetly named to coincide with his release but actually recorded before sentencing, was 'Out'.)

Prison life, or maybe the awful prison food, had taken its toll on Rob, but outwardly he looked awesome. He'd lost weight, his hair was shoulder length, and when he smiled I knew the old Rob was in there somewhere. Anyway, we had our mate back. With an irony we'd got used to, Simon Mayo was introducing that *Top of the Pops*. It was an amazing feeling to look to my left and see Rob back in his rightful place at his Hammond.

'Can't Get Out of Bed' had gone into the chart at No. 24. It had begun as a Small Faces-inspired instrumental, something that we felt could have been an outtake from their seminal album, *Ogdens'*

Nut Gone Flake, but we wanted to add vocals. We were recording in the Monnow Valley Studio. The rest of the band went home for the weekend, while me and Rob stayed to work on the vocals, with Dave Charles engineering. This was the first time the band had worked with Dave. He would become an integral part of The Charlatans – our sound, our attitude – and for me he is one of the most influential people I have ever worked with.

For the melody, Rob was thinking Bob Dylan — an idea that had perhaps come to him subliminally, as Dave Charles looked the spitting image of Bob – with a kind of 'Subterranean Home-sick Blues' rap-style vocal.

I was thinking John Lennon, 'I Am the Walrus', but maybe we had used that on 'I Never Want an Easy Life If Me & He Were Ever to Get There'. (Longest title in history? Maybe, but that's another story.) I had lots of words scribbled down over a few pieces of paper, but there wasn't any kind of order, so Rob just told Dave to 'Keep playing the track,' or 'Keep playing the song'; that's what he always did. I'm not sure whether he was really thinking of something or just playing for time, smoking constantly, smoking and listening. But that's what he did, and then he went into the vocal booth clutching the sheets of paper and he just went for it.

He did the first verse, with the melody that is on the record, but with my lyrics re-ordered to his taste.

I was in awe. It's the best memory I have of us two actually sitting down and pulling something wonderful out of barely nothing. We spent a few hours changing things round a little, getting the words to fit, and generally honing the song.

I wrote the bridge that evening, thinking about John and Yoko's 'bed-in', and Rob took the lead vocal: 'Can't get out of bed, you're keeping it straight, this city's a mess. Can't get out of bed, you're keeping it, keep on getting together.'

Pure Lennon! I get a spine-tingling feeling thinking about it now. It might be the best song we wrote together, a really great joint effort, but at the time we were unsure whether the euphoria came simply from the excitement of getting it finished. Only the two of us had heard it. But the feeling we had created was otherworldly, and I definitely got that now-recognizable sensation that tells me when something is right.

We told Dave to take the Sunday afternoon off so we could go fishing. Rob loved spending his time by the river, and he was showing me the ropes. It was great to spend time with him and connect with his softer side, which wasn't seen often on tour. It was a form of meditation for him, and we could shut out the pressures of the outside world, whiling away an afternoon at a river – not always by the rules recommended in the *Angling Times*, though: occasionally, elements of our other lives would be packed alongside the maggots. Whether our fellow anglers recognized the effects of ecstasy or just thought we were giddy, chatty and having the time of our lives catching fish was never discussed. Rob's impending trial was worrying him, and it was time away from it all.

The rest of the band started to trickle back to the studio that evening. We were really excited about them hearing 'Can't Get Out of Bed' for the first time. I remember being especially curious about what Martin would think. He wasn't a fan of Dylan or Lennon, but he loved The Small Faces. So surely he would love it? I just knew it, we knew it. He was bound to.

And yes, the reaction generally was rapturous, but especially from Martin. Everybody saw it as a breakthrough, and in a way we all thought, well, if Rob does go down, then at least this one should last us a while.

It was definitely the best song we had written up till now. But it was impossible to predict what the reaction of others would be. 'Weirdo' was a smash in America, while for some reason 'Can't Get Out of Bed' couldn't get arrested on the radio over there; in the UK 'Can't Get Out of Bed' was hailed as our best single yet and 'Weirdo' was monumentally slagged off, as was the album which it came from. We had given up on trying to guess what would be a hit though we would occasionally bump into the mainstream like meeting an old friend, not sure when we'd parted or if we'd ever be reunited.

Before we got to Monnow Valley, we had been demoing at Jacobs in Farnham, Surrey. We had recorded an instrumental of 'Can't Get Out of Bed' there and also made progress on tracks like 'It's Only the Music', which would later end up as 'Feel Flows', inspired by Parliament and Can, and 'I Never Want an Easy Life', another Small Faces-inspired 'soul' stomper.

About this time we were thinking again about who to use as a producer for the album. We had talked about Steve Hillage, not for his '60s psychedelic output with Gong, or his '70s solo prog musings, but for the work he had been doing with Primal Scream, System 7 and The Orb. We loved Steve, from his pure and honest eyes to his tales of acid-frazzled flashbacks. We gave him the job.

Mark was on fire. He had just bought a guitar from his mate Noel Gallagher, a Fender Jaguar. Noel didn't like the way it sounded, and probably needed the money too as this was 1993. Noel loved 'Can't Get Out of Bed', so much so that Oasis booked themselves into Monnow Valley to record their first lot of songs. But all that comes a little later in another story.

'I Never Want an Easy Life' was a song about Rob's impending court appearance, and the dual-lead vocal in the chorus meant, to me at least, that we were in this together. Perhaps the lyrics were about the twisted lives we were living. From the outside we looked fairly innocent – nice hair, happy smiles – but what was going on under the surface was a lot darker. We were trying to document it in the lyrics without being crass or too obvious, keeping our cards close to our chest.

In hindsight I guess we were all preparing for events to come – and under the circumstances I think we did well.

We finished off *Up to Our Hips* with Rob in prison. Unsurprisingly, our sound had moved away from our Hammond-driven past, and the album relied heavily on our new guitarist. Was it a direction we would have taken anyway? Who knows? It was out of our hands. We were nervous explaining to Rob how we had got Mark's brother, John, and a guy called Nigel to play keyboards while he was incarcerated. But he told me that he felt he had no right to have any kind of say in the band any more. It wasn't because of what he had done, it was what prison had done to him – it seemed to take away his self-confidence. Bandwise, he was a different person.

Martin instigated 'Jesus Hairdo', a Rod Stewart and The Faces-style good-time romp, featuring slide guitar, written, recorded and mixed in world-record time in Monnow Valley.

Last to be finished was 'Patrol', intended to be a Can/Blurt-style jam to ease in Mark's brother, John. It quickly became something special, more than just a song, a feeling! I finished the vocals for 'Patrol' and an earlier song from the four-month Monnow Valley album sessions – 'Inside-Looking Out' – in Chris Rea's Cookham studio, the Mill, in Berkshire.

I remember the mixing sessions and the vocal/lyric overdubs very well, because I was in love with a girl at the time. A girl called Chloe. And it was a big one!

★ ★ ★

'Compromise is the devil talking,' Kevin Rowland once said in the Dexy's song 'The Occasional Flicker'. He is right, of course. But then again, a lack of compromise can lead to an ill-advised Reading Festival appearance singing Whitney Houston's 'Greatest Love of All' wearing a man-dress while being stroked by stocking-clad dancers!

But certainly compromise often entails the best part of an idea being lost. One such case with The Charlatans was the sleeve of *Up to Our Hips*. I'd had the idea of using a picture from the 1960s by Lewis Morley – a timeless shot of a hairdresser and his model.

The idea was to re-create it with different people. A notable part of the original photo was the fact the guy in the picture wasn't wearing a shirt – our replacement, for some reason, wanted to keep his top on, and we went along with it. The only similarity between the final shot and the original is the number of people. Two. Everything else has changed. The models are too young, and at the time some people mistook them for the band. To me the sleeve looked like one for '80s band Dollar.

As bad luck would have it, *Up to Our Hips* was the first album released in the US without us having to be called The Charlatans UK (there had been two US bands before using our name) – with the shorter name and a boy and girl on the cover, lots of Americans were uncertain whether it was actually our band's new album.

To this day the sleeve is a regret. If I could change it to the original Lewis Morley photograph tomorrow I would, but we made the decision together. Later we would use Morley's classic shot of Christine Keeler for the cover of the single 'Tellin' Stories'. The use of that original cost us over £16,000 – thinking back, we should maybe have used Christine Hamilton and kept the difference!

You can see that it niggles me just writing about it. I do, however, always look for the positive in something, and that picture is my reminder that compromise isn't always the best way.

Now, where's my man-dress?

4. GARLIC BREAD AND BRITPOP

Britpop hasn't aged well. Its protagonists have hit middle age with a bump, from cheese making to making cheese and ill-fated reunion tours. Credible survivors are few.

Us? Do we get along? We're like a family. Does your family get along?

We are a functioning dysfunctional unit at times, but when it's good it's magic.

★ ★ ★

I first moved to London in 1990. I moved in with my girlfriend Sam, who I'd met in Steve's office at the record shop in Northwich. I fell for her straight away. She was gorgeous, with a confidence and class I hadn't seen before. She worked in music publishing, for Warner/Chappell in London, and she wanted to sign the band.

We would spend days watching films at the Gate Cinema in Notting Hill, stuff by Ken Russell and David Lynch. And *Paris, Texas*.

Perhaps I didn't realize it then, but at the age of 22 I had got the life I had dreamed of: a basement flat in Chiswick, a beautiful girlfriend who would bring home boxes of records, a kitten called Tipton and an ever-growing circle of people who just seemed to want to talk to me.

Chiswick felt permanently sunny and autumnal – it always reminded me of the opening scenes of *The Exorcist*. Mike Oldfield's theme would be playing on my internal jukebox. Nothing too dark had gone on yet – either with Ellen Burstyn or the newly cosmopolitan me.

Everyone tends to imagine that these times were a blizzard of cocaine, together with magnums of champagne and endless groupies, but we were much more innocent then – nothing stronger than beer fuelled us. The descent into large-scale drug-taking came later.

It seemed that everyone used to drop by our flat. Richey and James from the Manics, Andy and Loz from Ride, EMF, World of Twist, Intastella and Northside – with no announcement, just a knock at the door. The characters who made up the contents of the *NME* were gabbling excitedly in my little kitchen, drinking tea and looking for biscuits.

I'd moved to London because it was the dream, it's where everybody was, and I didn't feel as though I was deserting the North: I knew that I would always have Salford in my blood.

I was born at Hope Hospital and my grandma lived in nearby Swinton. Mum and Dad still live in Moulton. Don't go and try to find them – though I am sure they would make you a cup of tea.

And Manchester? Well, it never felt very far away, and in fact it wouldn't be too long before I was back there. And anyway it seemed that everyone from Manchester was in London.

Sam was my first muse and my confidante, she was the Suze Rotolo to my future wannabe Bob Dylan. As The Charlatans' publisher, she and I would be in this together.

I remember being alone with her when she got the phone call telling us that *Some Friendly* was No. 1. It was the best moment in my life. I knew straight away by the tone of her voice that she had just heard some good news. Though she was teasing me and trying to keep it from me, her smile gave it away. It really was the sweetest thing: 'You did it, baby, you're No. 1.'

The Charlatans were as much a part of Britpop as we were of Baggy – we didn't ask to be included, but it certainly helped us as TV executives and excitable journalists were falling over themselves for bands. At one time we appeared to fit into most genres that were kicking around – it certainly made for good times. Bands were being plucked out before they'd even recorded a note – bands like Menswear, whose styling came before their music.

★ ★ ★

Late '93 found me recording an episode of the infamous Channel 4 TV programme *The Word* with St Etienne, for the single 'I Was Born on Christmas Day'. I wasn't. I was born on 30 May 1967. I suppose your date of birth has to go in an autobiography somewhere, doesn't it? But this far in! Ah, well . . .

The Et's Bob Stanley *was* born on Christmas Day, though,

and he had suffered years of 'joint present hell'. He'd penned the song for me and Sarah Cracknell to sing.

Martin Kelly, a new friend who worked for Heavenly, mentioned that there was a girl he wanted me to meet, a girl with a beautiful voice. He said he'd fallen in love with her on the phone. Eventually he introduced me to Chloe – the porcelain-skinned Creation Records employee with the sparkling bushbaby eyes and the owner of the voice. She was standing with Alan McGee, and said in her Scottish brogue, 'I just told Alan to shut the fuck up.'

She seemed unafraid of abusing her boss. He seemed to like it, too.

I appeared on *Top of the Pops* with St Etienne, and afterwards we went back to Chloe's flat, where I would stay for about a year. We were sharing with Adrian Hunter, a gig promoter and, like me, a total music enthusiast. At the time of writing, Adrian is, among other things, Pete Doherty's manager. Also resident in the flat was Kleanthi Boutis, PR to Alan McGee at Creation. The final occupant was Kle's boyfriend, Stephen Duffy. Famed for an early audition with Duran Duran, and singer of the brilliant 1985 hit 'Kiss Me', his most recent successes have been as a co-writer and co-producer for Robbie Williams. Robbie had hooked up with Mark Ronson in 2007 to cover our song 'The Only One I Know'. Small world.

We were quite a bunch. We were in a cool flat above a pizza joint on Camden Parkway. There was a whiff of garlic bread and Britpop in the air.

It's hard to imagine now, but Camden then was arguably the most happening place in London. Like Shoreditch has been for the past few years, and like wherever next will be whenever. It seemed that everyone I was bumping into along the way was now in a band that was making waves. One day I was being introduced to my neighbour, a bookish young guitarist named

Bernard, the next day Suede were on the cover of every magazine. And from back home we could hear the distant squabblings of the brothers Gallagher.

In the flat we were all very close and were all shoulders to cry on when times got tough, weird or downright psychedelic. Chloe, Kle and I were together in the flat on 8 April 1994, doing nothing in particular, when Kle took a call from Gerry Love. Through the Creation Records set we were friends with Norman and Gerry from Teenage Fanclub. Gerry was ringing to pass on the news that Kurt Cobain had taken his own life. They had toured together, and the Fannies had been a huge influence on Nirvana's sound. It was two weeks after our album *Up to Our Hips* had come out and four months before the release of Oasis's *Definitely Maybe*. The tectonic plates of the music world were shifting.

Oasis played Glastonbury's second stage just before the release of their debut album. John Robb asked me if I was taking notes or picking up any tips. Cheeky git. Everyone used to call Liam 'Tim', just like everyone used to call me 'Ian' after the Stone Roses frontman. Tips? Maybe. After all, it's all about giving and receiving, isn't it? What you get you give back, just double the dose. You make it into your own.

Anyway, it was a strong performance from Oasis. I was a fan of the first album.

★ ★ ★

The Heavenly Sunday Social began on 7 August 1994 in the Albany pub on Great Portland Street and went on for thirteen weeks. I, along with just four others, went to each and every one. For me it had all the same traits, emotions and feelings as the Haçienda did, but it didn't go on long enough for the dark stuff to take hold. 'Life is Sweet' from the first Chemical Brothers album was the sound of the Albany. In some ways, though, the

Social was about keeping the tradition of Sunday evening intact – opening only from 6 till 10.30, which was pub closing-time back then.

There was also a broadsheet, a weekly update typed out by Robin from the Heavenly PR company. It was a new twist on the old idea of a weekly newspaper but specially for Sunday clubbers, available for free. People have tried to emulate it since, but this one was first.

Heavenly were to play a big part in our PR. Till now we'd been handled by Savage and Best, PR company of choice for the Camden set. Their office was right opposite where we lived, next to the Dublin Castle pub. Our manager Steve had appointed them, which was reasonable since they were the biggest name at the time. But when the Social started up I began having some informal conversations with the Heavenly people, which came to a head at a party at Robin's house in Shepherd's Bush after the last ever Sunday Social in November.

It was quite some party. The partners running Heavenly were Jeff Barrett and Martin Kelly. On this occasion I remember Jeff sitting glued to the stereo all night, with his hand on the volume control, forcing it up to number 11.

'Jeff, you gotta turn it down, mate.'

'Turn what down?'

'We can't fucking hear anything!'

The people in the flat above were pouring boiling water out of the window on us as we stood outside smoking, trying to get us to lower the noise, while Jeff was cranking up Stevie Wonder's 'Superstition' to full blast, out of his mind on E.

At some point during the party Martin told me how much he loved *Up to Our Hips*, but how bad he thought the press had been on it. In fact the press had been great – there just wasn't enough of it. He also said he was gobsmacked that our single 'Can't Get Out of Bed' hadn't been a huge hit that January. It had got to just No. 24. He asked me who did our PR and what they charged.

'20k,' I told him, and added sheepishly, 'It was our manager's idea.'

Martin said, 'You should let me and Jeff do it, we would do a much better job.' I was already feeling tempted – we seemed to be completely on each other's wavelength. 'And we would do it for 10k.' Deal!

I had to clear it with Steve, with the band and with our record company boss, Martin Mills, the smiling man of pop and a very savvy guy. For me it was a no-brainer, though from the outside it might have seemed crazy: Savage and Best, the PR company I wanted to leave, were the most successful in the country. But I felt we were moving to family: Heavenly's PR roster included Primal Scream, The Chemical Brothers, Andy Weatherall, Underworld and Beth Orton. They had the hippest and best club in Britain, possibly the world, and yet in some ways they were complete outsiders. They did things their own way.

We had a meeting round the dining table at Monnow Valley Studio, and it was agreed that I would ring Jeff the next day and get the whole business thing rolling.

Heavenly immediately began to do the press for the Boxing Day release of the single 'Crashin' In'. We all started to plot how to get The Charlatans back on track, though we weren't really sure how far off the track we were. Or which way things were going – but we sensed a musical sea change in the air.

Inspired by the goings on at the Social and the Camden scene, 'Crashin' In' was recorded in a weekend at Monnow Valley, with the idea of starting sessions for a new album. We recorded four songs and on a whim decided to release them straight away. Why fuck about? Let's do the show right here right now!

So 'Crashin' In', documenting the times, my times, our times, the Sunday Social times, was released on Boxing Day 1994, while everyone else was snoozing in their Christmas-cracker paper crowns.

I was in Glasgow with Chloe for Christmas. We headed for the HMV store on Sauchiehall Street and everyone was scrambling for the record, a good sign. The sleeve looked good; it was a great shot of the band on the street with a Hammond organ, an idea borrowed from the cover of The Beastie Boys' seminal album *Check Your Head!*, a favourite of ours at the time. The focus of their picture on the cover was a ghettoblaster; ours was a Hammond X-5. I got Tom Sheehan to take the photograph, and all of a sudden we'd had a much-needed makeover and we were back in the groove.

It wasn't much, but it was the shot in the arm we needed. We didn't get much radio play, just a few spots in the evening. Steve Lamacq and Jo Whiley were, as ever, very supportive. But still – no major radio airing.

Whatever it means to be played on 6 Music or Xfm in terms of record sales these days, at least there are those outlets. You can sit and listen to 6 Music and you can discover new sounds. In 1994 Radio 1 was as mainstream as it has always been, and Radio 2 was a golden oldies station. It hadn't started to become even vaguely credible. It's sometimes hard to remember the world without the internet; these two stations had a stranglehold on the airwaves then, and we fell somewhere in between the two.

'Crashin' In' sauntered in at No. 31. I wasn't unhappy. It was low, but it felt like we were at the beginning of something new. People were taking notice again.

* * *

Martin Kelly and I became inseparable at this time. I remember going to his flat in Ladbroke Grove and spending the whole evening talking about Bob Dylan. I was into Dylan, and getting in deeper. Martin pulled out *Biograph* and asked me whether I had it. I didn't. He played me 'You're a Big Girl Now', a version only available as part of this box set. Martin thought it was the best thing Dylan had ever done. He had two copies of *Biograph*, a CD and vinyl, and he generously gave me the vinyl. Mates for life!

As a result of our shared enthusiasm, Dylan's influence began to be heard in The Charlatans' sound. I had used him as a reference point as far back as 1991, with the song 'Happen to Die', but the more I listened the more I loved. Songs like 'Here Comes a Soul Saver' and 'North Country Boy' showed how Dylan was becoming further integrated into our music, via osmosis and many late nights. It was evident on our self-titled album and *Tellin' Stories* especially. I was aiming to bring an American '60s influence into what was being called Britpop.

It irritates me when we are described as the archetypal band for a number of different scenes. Were Baggy and Madchester one and the same? We apparently represented both. After that we were Britpop.

Oasis were all about The Beatles and T Rex. Blur were channelling Wire and The Kinks. As well as Dylan, I was completely absorbed by Gram Parsons and The Lovin' Spoonful, and discovering for the first time The Staples Singers.

We were on a roll again, and people were saying we were the new Rolling Stones. Did I believe them? Would you? I wanted to. The Stones had an American flavour, and me and Mark could definitely pull a Mick and Keith pose once in a while. We were outsiders, on the fringes of Britpop. Just like we'd been outsiders in the Madchester scene.

Anyway, I was happy. I was just glad that people were listening to bands again. And we were doing our own thing.

★ ★ ★

The first time I ever heard Gram Parsons was in 1993. Bobby Gillespie had given Chloe a copy of a CD called *Farther Along: The Best of the Flying Burrito Brothers*, and Gram was their singer. He referred to his country/soul vision as 'cosmic American music'. Not since New Order's *Power, Corruption and Lies* a decade earlier had a record floored me like this. I remember listening to it on repeat in Camden: drinking coffee and smoking Marlboro and observing an impromptu, uninvited, mouse-based floor show taking place by a hole in the skirting board while singing along to 'Cody Cody' and 'Christine's Tune'.

Another musical door had opened for me, similar to the one Crass had smashed open in 1979. Before Crass it had been The Buzzcocks and The Vibrators, and before them – thanks to Uncle Andrew – Peter Gabriel-era Genesis.

★ ★ ★

We were pretty close to Oasis, and our paths crossed on lots of occasions. Noel was a fan and we played a number of gigs with them. Our names were often linked, and we would run into them at the annual award bashes that magazines would throw. After the red-carpet entry it would be like some kind of indie music AGM. There were those who had given up drink while others had taken it up almost professionally, and gaggles were taking regular trips to powder their noses as others looked on disparagingly, the line becoming blurred as the night went on and the drinks were sunk.

I left Camden and moved a mile up the road to Chalk Farm, where I started writing for our fourth album. It was originally titled *First Shag in Ages*, after an Irvine Welsh quote. Some promos were even sent out with that title before we settled for the less controversial *The Charlatans* – though the vinyl retained the original name etched in the run-out groove as some kind of nod to nonconformity. I call it The Black Album.

Mark and I had just started our writing relationship together. Our songwriting honeymoon was a week's holiday with girl-friends on Spain's Costa del Sol, where we mapped out all our ideas while lying on lilos in the sun.

Creation was based in Primrose Hill, just over the bridge. Mark would visit for a week at a time, and we wrote 'Just When You're Thinking Things Over', 'Tell Everyone' and the begin-nings of 'Here Comes a Soul Saver'.

We bumped into Liam in the Pembroke Castle pub after he and Noel had had one of their heated debates, and he came back to the flat. We drank, shared stories, generally got all Mancu-nian, and we played him the latest track we'd been working on and had high hopes for – 'Just When You're Thinking Things Over'. We were really proud of it, and we thought he'd like the Lennon influence. Like some kind of Northern game of Top Trumps he pulled out a Maxell C90 and handed it to me, with the instruction, 'Stick this on.' We started to play it, and one of Noel's familiar guitar riffs rang out, followed quickly by some tambourine, pounding drums and Liam's declaration, 'Some might say that sunshine follows thunder'. Our song would hit the dizzy heights of No. 12 in the singles chart, but theirs would be their first No. 1.

Primrose Hill was also where Primal Scream had their studio, and I would often find myself there while they were recording their album *Vanishing Point* – Liam would also call in, as would lots of the bit-part players in that scene: Lisa Moorish from Kill City, Brendan Lynch, Paul Weller and My Bloody Valentines' Kevin Shields.

Chloe worked with a woman called Splash – a Canadian employee at Creation and one of my favourite people to hang out with. I'm not sure about exact job titles at Creation, and I'm pretty sure they aren't either. She was married to Dave Rown-tree, the drummer with Blur.

The Britpop juggernaut was hurtling along now. Oasis were approaching the peak of their powers, and Shaun Ryder and Bez were having a resurgence through Black Grape. Magazines outside music were picking up on the rising popularity, and it brought out a communal spirit which was at its height during the summer season of festivals. At T in the Park, after Kylie Minogue had played and then we had gone on, I was introduced to a familiar face, looking rather concerned. 'I think I've lost Bez,' were Joe Strummer's first words to me.

I've never been overly concerned whether people know what I do when I meet them, but the fact that Joe Strummer was aware that I was a singer in a band gave me a giddy glow, and although I had just walked off stage and given Kylie a peck on each cheek, those first few moments with Joe instantly became the highlight of my weekend, week, month, year. We ambled over to his transit van, chatting about nothing in particular, and Joe began rummaging through some plastic bags, sleeping bags and a weekend's worth of camping detritus. He was a seasoned festival-goer, and in one swift move he changed his boots and rolled a spliff, then off we went again.

Joe invited me to his campfire that evening, but unfortunately I had to be off to my next festival, with thoughts that some day I would take him up on his offer. Joe's campfires became festival legend, and Strummerville, a charitable foundation set up by his wife after his death, is a fitting legacy.

Joe's music had a profound impact on my musical life from the earliest days, and, as they say, the first cut is the deepest. My ever-changing top nine records would always have *Sandinista!* completing the ten.

It's a sprawling Hollywood epic, with a cast of thousands but starring Mick 'Bogart' Jones, Joe 'Travis Bickle' Strummer, a strung out Topper Headon, and a loucher than louche Paul Simonon. I bought *Sandinista!* from Woolworths in Manchester for £3.99, the price insisted on by the band, stopping CBS charging more. Imagine a time when bands had not only the power to insist on releasing a triple outing but also the clout to set the price!

It was an early Christmas present to myself, aged 13, and must have been the product of a lot of scrimping. The only other album of theirs I owned was *Give 'em Enough Rope*. Neither of these albums is considered their finest, but they are the ones that mean most to me. *Sandinista!* is my favourite Clash album for many of the reasons that some critics and fans were disappointed. I like its filmic, cartoon-like quality – it is genre-splicing, topical and brave. Critics, on the other hand, have called it patchy, pseudo-revolutionary and an unnecessary ego trip.

I'd first got to know of The Clash through my schoolfriend Panhead, who I assume these days uses the slightly more acceptable moniker of Peter Clews. He had two older brothers, Sticker and Tant, who unknowingly introduced me to:

Cockney Rejects – *Flares 'n' Slippers*
Tubeway Army – *Replicas*
Devo – 'Jocko Homo' and *Q: Are We Not Men?. A: We Are Devo*
The Stranglers – *Rattus Norvegicus*
The Jam – *All Mod Cons*
The Sex Pistols – *Never Mind the Bollocks*
The Clash – first LP plus the singles 'White Riot', 'Complete Control', 'Clash City Rockers' and 'White Man in Hammersmith Palais'

It was the summer holidays – isn't it always when you think back to childhood? – and Sticker and Tant were out doing important late-teenage stuff like getting into trouble, locating

magic mushrooms and going to early punk gigs. Mr and Mrs
Clews were out at work or down the social club, so me and Panhead would be listening to their sons' records.

Did I find *Sandinista!* immediately overwhelming? Not when
I was 13. I remember not being that impressed by The Beatles
either, but with both of these groups it would later dawn on me
how important they were.

When you buy an album and spin it for the first time, you
usually only have eight to twelve tracks to get to grips with. It's
a limited-overs one-day international. But *Sandinista!* was a five-
Test series. It had thirty-six songs, some of which didn't even
feature The Clash; lead vocals on a couple are taken by schoolchildren.

If thirty-six tracks is not enough to satisfy your appetite,
then check out Ellen Foley's mostly Strummer/Jones-written
album *Spirit of St Louis* (a.k.a., in some circles, The Lost Clash
Album) to get more.

The tracks on *Sandinista!* I took to first were the ones that
sounded most like the Clash of old: 'Somebody Got Murdered',
'Something About England' and 'Police on My Back' (an Eddy
Grant cover). 'One More Time' and 'Washington Bullets' would
come to me a little later, the latter being as political as anyone
had ever been in the mainstream. Then 'Ivan Meets G.I. Joe',
'Lose This Skin' and so on and so on, till I was telling anyone
who would listen that 'Midnight Log' and 'Junkie Slip' were as
good as anything they had ever done. They weren't, but with
such a monolithic release there were bound to be a few cracks.
With their ambition came flaws, but that was natural. I didn't
mind my triple LPs flawed, especially for £3.99.

To me this album is a blueprint of inspiration and bravery for
anyone who is in a band at the height of its powers. In 1980 The
Clash were a huge band, and the fact that they were prepared to

risk releasing this crazy, sprawling beauty will keep this LP in my Top 10 for as long as I live.

I found out later that 'Mescalero' Tymon Dogg, whose 'Lose This Skin' appears triumphantly on *Sandinista!*, was a musician mate of Joe's who Topper had bumped into in New York while they were making the album in Electric Ladyland. I went to see The Mescaleros on four consecutive nights at the Troubadour in LA, and it was a great excuse to hang out with Joe.

I was very fortunate to meet Joe on several occasions, and I spoke to him a few times over the phone while he was writing the words to a celebratory Manchester United song. I regret that I had no input in that, but as Mark had finished all his guitar parts for the album we were then putting together, whereas I was still up to my neck in it, I told him he should go to the recording session to represent the band. But the song was never released: United didn't make it to the final.

Joe did an interview on my behalf when he came backstage to the dressing room after a Charlatans gig in Reading. He was interviewed in the shower for a Radio 1 'On the Road with The Charlatans' piece by Emma Forrest. I had been documenting the tour for the BBC, and the Reading show would be the last entry. I bet they weren't expecting what they got, but what a great way to end!

Later I met and hung out with Joe every time he came to LA. He commented that the only fault with The Charlatans was the fact that there was no music in the dressing room. I think he saw something in us that we shared. I hope I am not being too vain in saying that there was a similar thread. Just like he was to everyone else in the world who likes music, he was a hero to me.

★ ★ ★

On 22 December 2002 I received a phone call from Neil Mather telling me he needed Tony Linkin's phone number. Tony was The Charlatans' PR at the time, and one of my best friends. Neil said he needed Tony's number before the news broke.

What news?

Joe Strummer died last night of a heart attack.

5. TELLIN' STORIES

Knebworth 1996 was as big as it could get. It wasn't The Charlatans' gig, it was Oasis's, but we, along with the most important bands of the time, played Knebworth. Oasis were obviously headlining, and Noel picked us, The Prodigy, The Chemical Brothers, Ocean Colour Scene, Kula Shaker, The Manic Street Preachers and The Bootleg Beatles to play with them. It was 250,000 people over two days in total, and what was hard for us was the fact that Rob Collins had died in a car crash a few weeks before we played it. It was our first gig post-Rob, the end of an era for the band, and potentially the end of The Charlatans: a disaster waiting to happen in front of our biggest audience yet. It was also the end of an era for Oasis, because how could they have got any bigger than that? But for us particularly the future was, to put it mildly, a little fragile.

Rob died in a car accident driving back to the studio from Monmouth town centre just before midnight on 21 July 1996. On that fateful Monday, his BMW slid off Rockfield Road and, after hitting several parked cars, flew fifty yards through the air before landing in a cornfield. Rob wasn't wearing a seatbelt, and he was thrown through the sunroof. But he wasn't killed instantly; he got up and staggered about for a while – an image that still haunts me today. He probably got to see his life flash before him, which is reassuring; I hope he had some nice thoughts among the dark ones.

During the weeks between Rob's death and Knebworth we had to work out whether we were going to continue. We had to cremate Rob. We had a lot of crap to sort out.

Bobby Gillespie from Primal Scream suggested that Martin Duffy could help us out. I remember taking a call at Monnow Valley Studio from Jeff Barrett telling me that, despite Rob's death, we had to do the gigs, and Duffy would play keyboards. I don't think Duffy was aware of any of this at the time, but he was being put forward by friends who knew we needed help. There were three concerts coming up: Loch Lomond on 4 August, Knebworth on the 11th and the V96 festival on the 18th with Paul Weller. I just didn't think it was possible.

We were numb and scared, but Jeff was persistent, telling me that we had to do the gigs: it was too important not to. He said it would be just like riding a horse after a fall: once we got back on we would be fine, it was just the first few hesitant steps that would be difficult. I loved Jeff for saying that. He didn't have to.

He was a big player in London, but he really came through for me. Without his nurturing and help, I wouldn't be here today. I could quite happily have not played those gigs and taken a long time off to recover from the blow of Rob's death, but they became the future, our future: the moment we would leave the past behind. We would do it and we would do it in glory, with true-grit Brit spirit and all that!

Loch Lomond, scheduled for just under two weeks after Rob's death, seemed too soon for a comeback. Even for Jeff. So we politely cancelled and began getting our heads together to begin what seemed like a mountain climb.

Duffy was our angel sent from London, via the Midlands. I had been a fan since his days in Felt, and he was now a fully paid-up member of the Scream team. I'd met him for the first time under a table backstage at a Charlatans gig in Amsterdam. We were both on E. Cypress Hill were passing round joints as big as the Camberwell carrot. The paranoia had got to me, but I didn't want to bail out and I think Duffy was hiding from his girlfriend, so I joined him under the table and kept him company. We clicked. I loved him and we just continued the conversation when I met him in the pub at Stone Station before rehearsing for Knebworth. It was natural. He was my hero.

We pulled it off: Knebworth was a great success. Yes, it was Oasis's crowd, but we were the band of the day, because it was so emotionally charged. I could really feel people willing us on. We arrived in a helicopter, which added a bizarre aspect to the already strange goings-on. There were two reasons for it. Steve said he wanted us to feel like kings (his exact words); and, more mundanely, there was the traffic. We were staying in a hotel miles away from the venue to keep us away from prying eyes and press attention, as everyone was really interested in how we would cope. We were car-crash TV waiting to happen. The band had just lost their keyboard player, arguably the most important member of the band, and we were going to come out and play in front of 125,000 people. What they didn't know, though, was that Martin Duffy, Rob's replacement, was a genius.

We all had dinner together in the hotel the night before the gig, and I remember watching *Later with Jools Holland* – it was shown on a big screen for us while we were eating. They replayed our most recent performance from *Later* and then, at the end of the programme, they broadcast in silence a picture of Rob for an entire minute. I was choked up. We all were.

When we landed at Knebworth, a TV crew came running towards us, saying, 'Tim, Tim, what's going on? Who are you most looking forward to seeing today?' To which I replied, 'Us.' I meant it. I wasn't being arrogant: it was euphoria. I was just ready. I wanted to see us go down in a blaze of glory or do ourselves the biggest favour and steal the show. I was so on edge, but I had nothing to lose now. I didn't know it then, but the whole of Knebworth were on our side before we even set foot on the stage. We were already in their hearts.

When Rob died, we were half way through recording *Tellin' Stories*, our fifth album. It was only Mark and myself who were in the studio on the night Rob died. The whole day afterwards was a blur. It was Jon Brookes who said, 'We can't split up on the morning of the 23rd July.' When he got to the studio we all agreed that that was the place to take care of business for the next few days. We all got together. We had reporters outside the window, local and national press. We had friends coming over to pay their respects, and Rob's mum, dad and sister came by, which was very hard to take in. I don't think Rob's mum ever got over his death, and for some odd reason Rob's dad seemed to take it all out on me. Maybe I said something weird in an interview? I know I had a different vision of who his son was from the one he had.

So we decided to carry on, to keep Rob Collins' name alive if nothing else, and we had to finish the record that would become *Tellin' Stories*. (We were going through an unexplained phase of dropping 'g's – which I suppose made a change from dropping Es.) We all agreed that we were making a really good record. 'One to Another' was already finished, while 'North Country Boy', 'Tellin' Stories' and 'How High' were written and almost finished, so the plan was just to go on.

But when I walked off the stage at Knebworth, I wanted to call it a day. The whole lead-up to the gig had been such an emotional time that when it ended I felt like the bubble had burst and the dream was over. I pretty much just sat at the side of the stage in tears. We all took a long time getting off the stage. Perhaps we felt it would be the last time we were all going to play together and were therefore savouring the moment. I remember hugging Mark and telling him how I felt, and he seemed to feel the same as me. So for at least ten minutes, or maybe an hour, or even the rest of the evening, we had split up and were no more. It was the end of the band . . .

I'm always on a high when I'm on stage, and the comedown from it is hard. But the two weeks leading up to this moment had taken an incredible emotional toll on us all: were we going to survive or were we not? My whole life I had wanted to be in a band, and at this point I was thinking it could go either way. But at least we pulled it off at Knebworth. The crowd were right behind us. It felt like the whole of Britain was behind us, really, and Oasis certainly were. Liam dedicated two songs to Rob that night. Rob had recently started hanging out with them quite a lot.

I spent a lot of time broken down in tears during the making of *Tellin' Stories*. Maybe the cocaine comedowns had something to do with it. But I was also coping with the fact that my long-time girlfriend Chloe had left me for some goon from Go! Discs record label, and though I got quite a lot of inspiration from how distraught I was it still didn't feel good at the time. Rob's death was the last straw, the worst thing of all. At his funeral, I was absolutely beside myself. Uncontrollable. Confused. And I really thought the eulogy was a joke. Were they talking about the same person?

Coming off at Knebworth, the first person I saw backstage was Ben Marshall, a journalist and supporter of the band, and he was crying his eyes out. He was accepting the loss, obviously – he had been to the funeral – but he also thought there was a future for us as well. He had to write a review, and he said, 'As I write this review with tears in my eyes, and I have seen the band over fifty times, I have never seen them so vicious and angry and passionate' . . . or something like that.

So I guess we lost something, but gained something else on that day. Courage perhaps, but maybe spite, too. Maybe we grew up in forty-five minutes in front of 125,000 people, or at least in those few weeks since Rob's death. I still get tingles down my spine and goose bumps remembering what we did. I think it was empowering. We got a weird energy from losing something irreplaceable. I felt like I'd lost a leg or an arm, but the great thing about having Martin Duffy in your band is the fact that he is probably the best keyboard player in Britain, or at least the most naturally gifted. He isn't like Rob in any way at all. Rob's playing was savage – he was a really angry musician – whereas Duffy is more classical, just beautiful, calm, naturally gifted. So he was completely different but, you know, the genius was there. Equal amounts of genius. And perhaps the key to all of this was the fact we didn't have time to think before we walked onto the stage, we just felt it.

Emotions were certainly at an all-time high. Rob's keyboard tech and habitual punchbag, John Clark, tried to get on the stage to pull Duffy off the organ mid-set, because he got it into his head that it was 'what Rob would have wanted' – one of the most dangerous phrases of that time. It can be a great sentiment, but it was overused and it exposed just how raw everyone's emotions were. Those words got me into many arguments. Who's to say what Rob would have wanted?

People went mental in the aftermath of Rob's death, reacting in such weird ways, but I think the way The Charlatans handled it was very dignified. Although, in reality, it took me about ten years to get over it. I still think about Rob every day. Ten years of self-loathing and ten years of self-medicating; but almost ten years to the day since Rob's death . . . I got clean.

★ ★ ★

The good thing about coming back to Rockfield, and going past the place where Rob died, is that I can now never be sure of the exact spot where the accident happened. It's really reassuring that, after fourteen or fifteen years, I only have a vague recollection of all the gory details, and I have none of the nightmares any more.

Guilt is a strange thing. For ten years, I self-medicated. The sessions at Monnow Valley were really messed up, mainly because of drugs. Rob had learned to make crack with bicarb and cocaine and to heat it in the microwave. I was into that, and I also found it really amusing when he spiked my tea with speed, just as I was going to bed at two in the morning, so that I wouldn't go to sleep for three days. I was the biggest drug-user in the band until Rob came out of prison; then we vied for the accolade.

There was no weirdness between us over drugs, but the rest of us managed to keep our shit together during sixteen-hour days, 11 a.m. to 3 a.m. But Rob was on a different schedule depending on what time he got back from the club in Bristol or the drug dealers in Swansea or London. That's why we had to

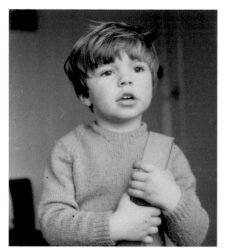

1. *Circa* 1969, Salford.

2. Claire, Dad, me and Mum – Bolton Road, Pendlebury, early '70s.

3. Paternal grandparents Madge and Eddie, Bolton Road, Pendlebury, 1979. Around this time I went to my first gig.

4. Maternal grandparents Agnes and Albert at my mum and dad's in Moulton, 1982. I really miss them.

5. Seventeen years old, with my first car, a Triumph Dolomite 1600. Behind it, my dad's Austin Ambassador.

6. With manager Steve Harrison, backstage in Leeds, 1990.

7. Jon Baker, Rob Collins, Jon Brookes, Martin Blunt and me.

CH_1020_02.tif

CH_1020_04.tif

CH_1020_10.tif

CH_1020_11.tif

CH_1026_16 .tif

CH_1026_18.tif

CH_1026_20.tif

CH_1026_22.tif

CH_1026_24.tif

CH_1026_26.tif

CH_1026_28.tif

CH_1026_30.tif

CH_1026_32.tif

CH_1026_34.tif

CH_1026_36.tif

CH_1026_38.tif

8. Photographer Ian Tilton asked me to move around a bit. I went for every pose
I could think of.

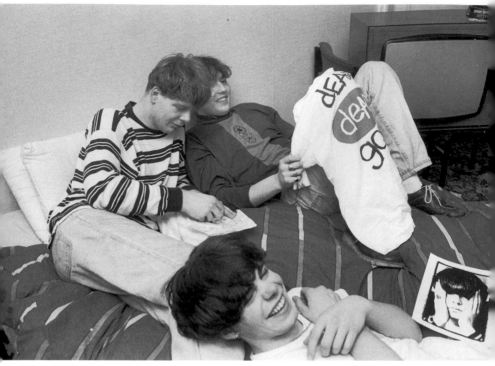

9. Jon Baker, Rob Collins and me. The band would be given one room after a gig, and this is often how we used to sleep.

10. 1991, moving away from the bowl haircut. Not sure where this was though: either King George's Hall, Blackburn, or Japan!

THE FACE

No 25/OCTOBER 1990 £1.50 • US $4.95
ITALY L5500 GERMANY 10.60DM SPAIN 435PTAS BELG. 105 BFR

SPIKE LEE, INC.
The empire strikes black

LEEDS RISING
Raves and raids
in West Yorkshire

**HELL'S
CHILDREN**
Clive Barker writes

NENEH CHERRY,
SINEAD O'CONNOR
GO RED HOT & BLUE

TIM BURGESS photographed by Julian Broad

THE CHARLATANS
SEXIER THAN SHAKY ?

PLUS
JULIAN CLARY
ROBIN WILLIAMS
JULIA ROBERTS
JANET JACKSON
BIKERS
TWIN PEAKS

11. & 12. *The Face* – until its demise, my favourite magazine. I was really proud of this cover. The dove represents peace and freedom. It was also the name of the best Es around at the time.

13. Me, Jon Brookes and Mark backstage in Chicago, 1992 –
the *Between 10th and 11th* era.

14. At a festival in Washington,
DC, 1992.

15. Mark Collins, North Country Boy.
This is a polaroid taken in 1996, with
Mark posing as Dylan on the 1969
Nashville Skyline cover.

16. Michelle and me at the Roosevelt Hotel, Hollywood, on New Year's Eve, 1998. The photo was taken by Harry the Dog.

17. Joshua Hayward and me at the back of The Horrors' tour bus, in a photo taken by Faris Badwan.

18. The band at the 2010 V Festival, posing for *NME* photos in Hylands Park.

19. On stage at the O2 Academy in Liverpool, 2010.

20. The New Village Charter High School, Los Angeles. I did a talk for
the David Lynch Foundation about transcendental meditation, My Drug Past . . .
and life in general.

employ another engineer just for him, because he would want to record whenever he felt like it. Ric Peet was that engineer, and he and John Clark were his cohorts, and they would do whatever he wanted and get him whatever he wanted, whenever he wanted it.

But as the sessions went on, the songs which Mark, Martin, Jon and I had worked on in the daytime began to get butchered in the early hours. Songs Rob didn't like he would ruin on purpose, and songs he did like he would ruin because he was so fucked up. Two days before Rob died, I had a huge argument with him, possibly about Ric Peet, I can't really remember. He stormed off, got into his red BMW and went home.

Over the next couple of days I confided in Mark, and I pretty much said that Rob had to go. We had been recording for seven months at this point, making the follow-up to *The Charlatans*, our second No. 1 album, which had taken us just four months to record. I said, we can't have him in the band any more. I had to check myself to see that this wasn't all just a huge ego thing on my part, wanting rid of our star player. But he wasn't our star player at the time or, to be honest, at the time of *The Charlatans*. Mark and I were the stars then.

6. 2–0 TO MUSIC

Throughout my time with The Charlatans I have always had a girlfriend, and for twelve years a wife. I never saw the music as a fleeting thing, so I never saw the need to go round grabbing what I could – some people see their time in the business as a kind of sex 'n' drugs trolley dash, doing as much as they can before it comes to an end. I was in it for the long haul.

And anyway, I'm a terrible liar! My face goes red when I'm not telling the truth. But that's not to say I would do any of that sort of thing even if I was an accomplished fibber – I just wasn't built for it. I won't deny that I have had some sexual encounters with friends who made it available to me with no strings attached when I was girlfriendless and at a loose end. After all, what are friends for? With friends who offer you casual sex, at least you know where you stand.

But I have always been sensitive to heartbreak and the feelings associated with a broken heart, and I wouldn't want to do to someone what I couldn't handle being done to me. I can't imagine a lonelier feeling than watching a person whose name you can't recall awkwardly leaving your hotel room. And the thought of someone using musical achievement (or actually no achievement at all!) as a means to some kind of conquest really turns me off.

I always wanted to be in love, and enjoyed nothing more than the experience of falling in love; the idea of losing that for the immediate gratification provided by a post-gig encounter was just unthinkable. (My first tutoring in the world of rock 'n' roll came from the school of Crass and, in particular, their album *Penis Envy*, which carried the message that women were to be respected, not sex objects to be exploited. The album was sung, written and performed by women and a boy named Penny.)

Some people do join a band to improve their sex life – girls can't resist a narcissistic frontman, all ego, sweat and leather trousers, with whom to pursue their rock 'n' roll fantasies. I was too in love with the idea of love and being in love. Like when Groucho Marx proclaimed that he wouldn't want to be a member of any club that would have him, I wouldn't want to be the crush or sexual fantasy of anyone who would throw themselves at the singer in a band.

Not that I didn't run into trouble sometimes. Customs in Japan for example can be a little confusing. On one occasion I was led to my room by a girl who I presumed worked for the promoter or our label. She escorted me to the door, and I naively thought she was coming in for some kind of tea ritual or maybe a late-night shoulder massage. Nope. She whipped off her clothes and jumped under the covers. I was beside myself worrying that she'd thought that I'd been expecting to spend the night with her. She gathered up her stuff and scuttled out when I explained I had a girlfriend and it wasn't something I did. By chance she ran into someone else who was more accommodating. He was late for the pick-up the following morning, getting treatment for his newly acquired genital companions. Music was now at least 2–0 up. Even acting as my guardian when needed.

Still, most autobiographies these days deal with titillation and scandal – the museum of rock 'n' roll revolves around the classic threesome of sex and drugs and rock 'n' roll, and I will try not to disappoint you. Except that I've always been into the idea of being a one-woman man. Sounds like a song? Not sure how much of a hit it would be, maybe a B-side? Anyway, I suppose it would go like this:

Verse 1: Girl from Northwich

My first serious girlfriend before I joined The Charlatans was a local girl from Northwich. I was in a band with her, we went to see bands together, and we shared intimate personal parallel lines. And I don't mean drugs. This was way before I was serious about drugs, when I was just an inquisitive, cheerful, sweet boy.

Actually she may have been my third or fourth love but, like Prince Charles said, it depends on what your definition of love is. I seem to fall in love quite easily. Jenny Agutter may have been the first, in *The Railway Children*; maybe my babysitter from next door too; and Farrah Fawcett!

I now believe she realized my calling to be in a band way

before I did, as she was the first girl who hit me with the ulti-matum – it's me or the band, Tim. It was 1-0 to music, of course, even though my nameless band were never going to save the world like Bono or Geldof were (this was Live Aid time).

1-0 to music perhaps, but by no means would this call for a lap of honour. I was devastated. But these are the sacrifices you have to make if you are serious about what you're doing, even though I had no idea just how serious I was. My dad always thought I was very serious, as I spent all my pocket money and money earned from various jobs on music-related things – records, guitars, keyboards, vocal PA and microphones. And I seemed to be in bands all the time, organizing rehearsals and picking up other band members. I was quite often the only one who could drive, and I would end up loading all the gear back into my mum and dad's at the end of the night.

I put in the miles. I had been bitten by a bug – not the bug of fronting a band but the love of seeing what music did to people. I never for one minute thought I would end up fronting a band.

Verse 2: Girl from London

I met her in our manager's office. She had a cool aura. She was from Harrogate but lived in London. She had her feet on the table in the meeting when I first walked in. I liked that.

She signed the band to Warner/Chappell Publishing. I really liked that.

And she came with me to Charlatans gigs as often as she could. That was good, too.

Together we moved into a basement flat in Chiswick. We went to gigs together and she taught me a lot. She taught me about the films of David Lynch and took me to see *Blue Velvet* in

Notting Hill. From this romance a love of cool independent films stays with me: *Wings of Desire, The Unbearable Lightness of Being, Betty Blue, Monsieur Hire* and *The Hairdresser's Husband.* And many more.

She took me to the launch party in Prestwich for the Fall album *Extricate*. I was superexcited, as The Fall were a long-standing favourite band of mine. This was definitely a highlight in my life so far, as I got to meet Mark E. Smith and we got on well.

She also took me to the Underworld in Camden to celebrate the launch of a new label called Heavenly. The bands that played that night were St Etienne, The Manic Street Preachers and East Village.

I remember the day she brought home *Disintegration* by The Cure and *Nevermind* by Nirvana. These were important records. This was an important relationship.

Our split was heartbreaking for us both. The band was starting to do really well, and I was distracted – it's what I'd always wanted and it took all of my attention. I decided not to come home immediately from a tour we were on, and took a train from Berlin to Paris, where I stayed for a week.

She was waiting for me when I finally got home, and we both felt we knew what was for the best. Neither of us could have predicted how difficult things had become. At the beginning we didn't know how long the band would last or how long we could last. But I do know that she helped and encouraged me to follow my dreams. And anyway, this book wouldn't be this book without a few tears.

I left Chiswick and bought a flat in Salford, close to where I was born and within walking distance of the Haçienda. Mark and I became inseparable. I lived on toast, painted the whole flat red and watched *Twin Peaks* on rotation.

Manchester's music scene was having another boom. It was during this time that I met Sarah Cracknell, and we would later go on and record a song together. And then I met the next important love in my life.

Now for the Chorus:

> I am in love with the idea of being in love,
> I am in love with the idea of love.

Verse 3: The Girl from New York City

I was standing at Crewe station and I was really down about something. Being down is not good, being down at Crewe station is terrible. Funny thing is, I thought to myself, I bet no one else at this station is going out with a hot girl from NYC.

It really cheered me up. I started to smile.

I had moved back in with Mum and Dad, records in boxes, belongings in bin-bags, head in tatters. But at the end of the road was a red telephone box, and every chance I had I would call The Girl from New York City. Northwich to New York seemed like a long way. It is.

The band were in between the second and third albums. We'd had one No. 1 album, but the follow-up had been less successful. Actually, it went into the charts at 21, and had it been our first album we would have been happy. But it was doing well in the States, and so was the single from it, 'Weirdo'.

Sam Bayer was drafted in by our US record company, RCA. Fresh from directing the video for 'Smells Like Teen Spirit', he would fulfil the same role for 'Weirdo'. He was funny, long-haired, loud and American. I remember after one of the run-throughs Sam jumped up, whipped off his shirt, and yelled out, 'YEEEEEHAAAAAH! The Charlatans! You guys rule! Who the fuck are Nirvana?'

For all I know he said that at every video shoot, but at that moment I was going to accept it. The band collapsed laughing – we were tight, with lots of in-jokes, and shared the enjoyment of what we were doing.

I had known the hot Girl from NYC since the band first walked into her office in Manhattan in 1990. Three years later, after seeing her intermittently and most memorably at the My Bloody Valentine show at the Ritz on 11th street between 3rd and 4th, I flew into the city specially to see her.

As I fell head over heels in love with New York, I fell head over heels in love with her.

> I am in love with the idea of being in love,
> I am in love with the idea of love.

Verse 4: The Girl from Creation

I met her backstage at *The Word* in 1993 after performing 'I Was Born on Christmas Day' with St Etienne.

She was from Glasgow but was working in the Hackney office of Creation Records. It's odd, but I feel as if as soon as I met her I never left her flat in Camden, the one she shared with Adrian, Kle and Stephen, though I must have been commuting between Camden and Berkshire – we were mixing *Up to Our Hips* at Chris Rea's studio in Cookham.

We instantly became inseparable.

I was 27 and she was 21. People would ask us all the time when we were going to get married. One day in the autumn of 1994 she announced that she had found us our perfect Woody Allen apartment – we were both big fans of Woody. The building at the bottom of Eton College Road in Chalk Farm reminded her of the apartment in *Manhattan Murder Mystery*, which had come out the year before. It was beautiful.

I am in love with the idea of being in love,
I am in love with the idea of love.

Verse 5: LA Woman

I met Michelle in Los Angeles. She had the most beautiful brown eyes, the most beautiful skin I have ever seen, hair that smelled of sunshine, hands and feet made out of poetry. In every way she was pretty much damn near perfect.

The Charlatans were in LA to play at the Troubadour in June 1997, staying in the Le Parc Suites Hotel. On our arrival I received a fax from Ed Simons from The Chemical Brothers: 'Hi, Tim, would you please put Michelle Wilkins + 1 on the Guest List. She would love to come to the show.'

So I did.

Back in the hotel after the gig I spoke to her for the first time. We were listening to the new Wu-Tang Clan album, *Forever*, a sprawling double-CD masterpiece, and I was bouncing from wall to wall, being a full-colour animated version of myself.

My DJ mates Jon and Dan from FC Kahuna were on tour with us, and I figured she was their friend as I couldn't see any other connection, and we hadn't been formally introduced. By the end of the night, after exhausting myself from all the bouncing, I thought that I would show a little more interest. It turned out that she really was Ed's friend.

'Hi, Tim, so what do you think of the new Wu?'

'Pretty good. Though I think I prefer *Cuban Linx*.'

Only Built 4 Cuban Linx is a solo album by Wu-Tang member Raekwon the Chef. I'm not sure whether I really did prefer it, but I wanted to let her know that I knew my hip-hop. She was from Atlanta and she was sporting a gold tooth, and I can be a bit like that about my music.

She didn't seem very impressed with my hip-hop know-how, though, and launched at me with . . .

'Pretty good?! Fuck you, Tim Burgess. This is kick ass!'

A year later we were married.

The second time I saw Michelle, she was with Mark. Mark was the late-nighter in the band, and like all classic rock guitarists he would set up the party in his room. Michelle's + 1 on this occasion apparently got a little too close to Mark, and Michelle, being the protective, idealistic, Southern-girl type and all, told her friend to hightail it and leave. She was watching out for her new friend, and she knew Mark had a girlfriend and kids back home in Manchester.

Mark was in that helpless, drunken, 'This is my room, I don't have to go anywhere except the toilet' state. Occasionally he would close his eyes and then next minute he would jump off the bed to change the CD. Then he would sit back down on the bed, light up a cigarette, talk a while, then nod off. Definitely not on high enough alert to work out whether he was being hit on or not.

In December 1997 we were getting ready to play the Docklands Arena. Mark told me that Michelle was on her way to see us; was trying to get to the show before we started the first song.

That evening we slept together. Not in a sexual way but in a drunken pile, three in a bed, all with our clothes on. But I must admit we were getting closer, and I did secretly wish that we could have been alone to chat. I got the feeling, though, that she didn't want to be left alone with me.

I suppose I came across as a right suave charmer or maybe a bit of a cock. I did think I was the king of the castle that night in my hotel suite, as people who are a bit of a cock tend to do. She'd insisted that Jon Campy, one half of the Kahuna DJs, slept in my room, too; she would not be left alone with me. I guess I was a mess. And I had a girlfriend too.

Our show at the John Anson Ford Amphitheater was possibly my favourite Los Angeles gig ever. The venue is set up off the Cahuenga Pass, a natural amphitheatre surrounded by cypress trees, with roaming deer peeking over the edge when we were soundchecking. It was beautiful.

After the gig our tour manager ushered me into a little backstage room. Michelle was in there with her friend Randy Billings, part of the fabric of underground LA. I asked her whether she'd enjoyed the show. She said that the new song 'The Blonde Waltz' was incredible and it reminded her of Woody Guthrie.

I was in love! I was gobsmacked that she had immediately picked up that, since the last time I'd seen her, I had made the natural progression from owning over 100 Bob Dylan bootlegs to discovering and welcoming with open arms the entire back catalogue of the dustbowl blues pioneer Woody Guthrie.

I had always fantasized that one day I would entice and seduce a beautiful girl with my record collection. As a teenager I kept my records next to my bed, the most impressive ones to the front, i.e. the most obscure ones or the ones with the best sleeves. In my dreams I imagined a girl coming to my room, seeing my records, flicking through them, falling in love with my record collection and then of course falling in love with me.

Now maybe this was the girl. I was in my thirties and my musical knowledge was in my head rather than next to my bed, but still . . .

Once we were alone I just didn't want to let her out of my sight. She drove us to Le Parc in West Hollywood, the gay area of Los Angeles. (The Charlatans stayed there so often that some people thought we were a gay band.)

I invited everyone to my room, the band, the crew, Jim our security guy. We all danced to The Beach Boys, drank champagne, smoked a little pot. It really was as good as it sounds. My memory whisks me right back there: the golden smog, the

ocean breeze and the smell of the jasmine in the evenings under-
neath the red skies.

After a few hours, Michelle and I found ourselves alone again.
By this point we must have been sending out clear signals,
because all at once everyone seemed to look at us, smile and say
goodnight.

I asked her if I could kiss her, which was pretty cheeky since
I was going out with somebody back in England, but I was hyp-
notized, I saw a sparkle in her eye. She said yes!

At this point I am reaching for the Do Not Disturb sign to
hang on the door. We won't be down for breakfast and will
catch up with you in the afternoon.

So it started with a kiss and we ended up in bed, immediately
and half jokingly planning out our future. It was wonderful,
though far from certain. I'd realized though that if I didn't act
this time we would probably never see each other again.

And it felt like a good thing.

Next on my agenda was a Charlatans tour of Japan, and then
it was back to Manchester to break the news to my then girlfriend of two years.

It was Bob Dylan who was to soundtrack the beginning of
our love. 'Mama, You've Been on My Mind' and 'I Want You'
were the two songs in particular I remember from my first visit
to see Michelle in her apartment on Lanewood Avenue. I'd been
in Manchester for a week following our most successful tour of
Japan yet. I called her every day while I was away and faxed her
funny sketches of us holding hands and diagrams of where we
were going to live.

We were always going to live in either London or Los Angeles,
but in the end I figured why move Michelle to London when I
was going to be constantly going on tour anyway? And she had
many friends in LA.

Above her sofa in the living room of her flat she had draped a black sheet and made a black wall like a homemade indoor tent. Inside were Bob Dylan lyrics top to bottom, hundreds of them. She'd printed them all off at work and made us a lyric tepee.

She worked at the Rutter Group in the Valley, a company that supplied law books to attorneys all over the US. She would drive to the offices every day, always late, in her beat-up Mazda sports car. She drove without fear and without concern for the consequences, the fastest and scariest driver I have ever sat with. But she was alert, and strangely I always felt safe with her.

The first bar we went to after I'd arrived in LA was a place called the Lava Lounge. I walked in and was served by a guy in a Manchester United shirt. Not that unusual, I suppose, but it made me feel at home. He recognized me and told me he had once won a competition to travel with The Charlatans on our tour bus to Vegas. I remembered him then, he was paralytic and puked up in the back lounge. I had to tidy it up! Oh yes, I remembered him!

I flew back to Manchester and began working with the band on *Us and Us Only*, while Michelle stayed on at Lanewood. We were making the record in Middlewich, a beautiful village in Cheshire, beside a canal and not far from the Jodrell Bank radio telescope. It was to be our new base.

Us and Us Only was the first album made in our brand-new recording studio, the Big Mushroom – named on the day we found out our accountant had stolen £300,000 of the band's money. We went to the pub across the road, where a guy went into his bag and pulled out a seriously big mushroom. Not a magic mushroom – on that day everything seemed to be particularly unmagic.

7. LA WONDERLAND

I was at a party round at Martin Kelly's flat on Elgin Avenue, Notting Hill, during the 1995 Carnival. I was up a tree, smoking a cigarette and drinking beer with John Niven. He was working for London Records at the time, and they were interested in signing The Charlatans. He has since found fame as the author of one of the best books about the music business, *Kill Your Friends*. I was really keen to work with someone I liked and

admired. I felt that he understood me, and he enjoyed the pleas-
ures of tree-based drinking and smoking.

John knew the ballpark figure he would have to offer to sign
the band, but it wasn't just about the money. John was offering
us the chance to be on their Decca label, most famous of course
for being where Oasis took the idea for their logo . . . and for
The Rolling Stones.

We were ready to leave Beggars Banquet. It's not that we had
any animosity towards them, just that we were changing. We'd
made three No. 1 albums and Mark Collins was still sleeping
on a blow-up bed in a shared flat in Stockton Road, Chorlton.
(The alleged venue, incidentally, of a tryst between a certain
world-famous singer and a Stone Roses crew member.) And he
had a kid on the way.

Steve Harrison had MCA ready with a cheque in their hands.
But my loyalties were to Heavenly. I wrote a note in biro: 'Dear
Jeff, I promise to sign to Heavenly Recordings.' I felt that it was
meant to be – Heavenly were already looking after us artistically and press-wise. My handwritten note is up on the wall at
the Heavenly Social on Little Portland Street, and it might as
well be written in blood.

But you don't always get what you want. The band had five
members and a manager, and there were conflicting views as to
what should happen for the best. Some wanted security, the
manager wanted cash, I was responsibility-free and just wanted
to work with friends. And although Decca and John Niven were
very appealing, especially to me and Mark, I am not sure
whether a deal was formally offered.

It was felt, too, that Heavenly might not have the resources
for our ambitions. In my opinion Jeff, Martin and Robin were
pioneers – as well as doing PR they had always released records.
I'm not sure whether 'ambition' came into their remit. What

they did, they did naturally. They were cool precisely because they weren't self-conscious about what they did.

I had already pledged my allegiance with my hastily written note, but unfortunately there was more to consider than simply doing what I wanted. So promise gave way to compromise. It was agreed that we would sign with Universal – or was it MCA then? Hold on, it may have even been MCA Universal. Record companies are among the most corporate organizations in the world and bands the least so, so the working partnerships can be bizarre, to say the least. Like some kind of music food chain, labels, imprints and companies are eaten up, spat out, merged and severed with monotonous regularity. Deals were done like playground football-card swaps, and bands were like kids in divorces while the takeovers went on – one minute fought over and loved; the next, abandoned and out in the cold. It was important for us to have as much stability as possible, and that's what MCA and/or Universal offered. Kind of.

Back to the tree . . . It's one of my favourite places in the whole world to hang out, though it never used to be like that. When I'd moved with my mum and dad to the village of Moulton, after my first day at school I went to a place referred to by the locals as 'the swamp', which boasted the big three of frog spawn, mud and a rope swing. I climbed my very first tree, a huge oak, and I made it to the top without looking down. At the highest point, though, tremendous fear came over me, an overwhelming sense of panic. The thick trunk had given way to ever-thinning branches, and it suddenly dawned on me how precarious my position was. The gang I was with went to find my mum, which was a little humiliating but not quite as bad as not being able to move. I was frozen stiff with fear.

I was talked into a calculated descent involving a few small steps for this young boy but one giant leap for my future desire to be centre stage. Slowly and gingerly I was guided down.

When I touched the ground I felt like I had landed a plane after being talked through it, like in a '70s disaster movie.

Afterwards my dad told me that I couldn't be afraid of heights because he had climbed the Matterhorn and my mum had conquered Snowdon. So climbing must have been in my DNA, and soon I was charging up trees like a frustrated baboon in a safari park.

I'm not sure if everyone views their childhood with blind fondness, and the number of autobiographies based on abuse and neglect makes me think otherwise. My childhood is a blur of Christmases, birthdays, chocolates and relatives. And then some days of weird silences around the house with no explanation. I later discovered that I was being spared the news that a neighbour had committed suicide, or that Mrs So-and-So from over the road had walked out on her husband after going out for a pint of milk.

I was totally sheltered from the more problematic aspects of life in the big world. It was such a safe environment that, when tragedy did strike, it seemed to hit all the harder. I was in awe of a kid at school. He was the best rugby player and also the hardest kid in our year – another 'cock of the school', as he would be known in the '80s in the northwest. After school we continued playing rugby, but we would see each other only at the weekends. Weeks passed and I saw less and less of him, and then I heard he was ill. He was undergoing chemotherapy, but we held out hope as he seemed like the strongest kid we knew. After several months he knocked on the door and asked my mum if I was in. He was on crutches after losing a leg to cancer. We laughed when I told him he looked more punk with his bleach blond hair. We spent an afternoon talking music and shared a cigarette. I returned the copy of Generation X's 'King Rocker' I'd borrowed from him. It was the last time I'd see him alive. He died before reaching 18.

Some days just feel heavy with grief even before the news hits you. Like the day John Lennon died, there seemed to be something that everyone knew but me. Later that year I was getting a little more daring, and I persuaded a kid called Ollie, who I was hanging around with, to give me my first tattoo. Now it's barely a mark, but at the time it seemed like the most daring thing ever. And then someone from school ran up to me and told me that there'd been a car accident and Ollie had been killed. Gruesome details, like the fact he had been decapitated, deepened the shock. In those days, bereavement counsellors didn't exist and we were left to our own devices to deal with things. Most of us showed little reaction, but I could see sadness in the eyes of kids who didn't seem to have a care in the world a couple of summers before.

I remember climbing half-way up a sycamore tree in the orchard that stood a little up the road from where I lived. I was alone and it was the summer of 1978 – not quite as hot as the famous summer of 1976, which had had its hosepipe bans and heightened stress levels for the car-cleaning obsessives, but it was a hot one nonetheless.

For my birthday meal in May 1976 I'd ordered soup of the day and a knickerbocker glory. I had to kneel on the chair to get to it because the glass was so tall. On my birthday in 1978 I had slightly more of a landmark experience, my first orgasm.

I loved the tactile qualities of a tree climb. You could almost feel its heart beat, so strong was the sense of the tree as a conscious organism. As I climbed to the top of these beautiful living things my friends would look up and ask how it was up there. I watched people gently passing by, girls drifting up and down the path in floaty dresses and skirts. I remember the smell of their hair and perfume. I was dreaming about gold and I was dreaming about treasure. I thought about getting my ear pierced and wanted to be a pirate scaling a palm tree with a knife in my mouth.

I have no idea why these thoughts were in my head, but as I hugged the cool tree in the warm summer I noticed something going on in my shorts. I'll spare you the details, but from then on things were different. The girls at school, who had previously bored me or had been targets for dead arms or Chinese burns, were now viewed in a different light. I became shy around them but couldn't take my mind off them.

I reckon life is made up of two kinds of people: ones who climb to the top of the tree and those who are just happy to sit and chat and hang out at the bottom. Then when I think about it properly, I realize it's not quite that simple.

★ ★ ★

We delivered *Us and Us Only* in 1999. I think it really stands up well, but it was never meant to be commercial, it was meant to separate us from the Britpop pack, which it did. If *Tellin' Stories* was our *Blonde on Blonde* (it wasn't, but just pretend it was!), then *Us and Us Only* was our *John Wesley Harding*: detached and a step sideways. Perhaps difficult to promote.

But we were a new band now after all – we had to face life without Rob. Tony Rogers was our new keyboard player. He was a songwriter and contributed to the writing from the outset. Ironically, the loss of Rob had led to a new lease of life for the band.

I guess that shows the true strength of a group. Anyway, Universal promoted *Us and Only Us* really well, but it wasn't the record they wanted and neither was our next, *Wonderland*. We made *Wonderland* without the label even knowing, in a dark room on a steep hill just off Laurel Canyon. I desperately wanted it to do well in America, so we really went for it.

I was living there now and I wanted our records to succeed in my hometown, Hollywood, LA. I thought about every aspect of the album with that in mind: where it would be written, its title, who would produce it, and so on. I have some of the best memories ever of Mark and myself, writing 'Love to You' and 'Right On'.

It was all very inspiring, soul-stirring, Curtis Mayfield stuff! Warm evenings on my balcony at La Punta Drive, or La Punta Heights, as my mate Randy christened it, drinking margaritas and doing rail after rail of LA's finest white powder. We immersed ourselves in the city and let LA take over; it became just as much part of the album as the songs or any of us.

The drugs were a very big part of it: LA coke, lots of it, dealers at the house 24/7. We never ran out. And the environment changed the sound, the sun flooded in, the shutters were open and the ideas were flowing. It's an incredibly optimistic album.

The thing about going to Los Angeles to make a record was that, in my head at least, LA is everything from Brian Wilson and The Beach Boys to Gram Parsons and The Flying Burrito Brothers, The Byrds, Sly and The Family Stone, Rick James. It's as broad as the Manchester sound, and beyond. It's a big palette musically to draw from, and when we headed out to LA as a band, we were thinking along the lines of funk, soul and disco with possibly some country-inspired inflections on top of that.

We had Daniel Lanois come down to play pedal steel on 'A Man Needs to Be Told', which was quite a trip. Through his work with U2 I knew who he was, but I was now actually paying even more attention, because he had just produced Bob Dylan's Grammy-winning comeback album, *Time Out of Mind*. Jim Keltner, who had worked on the same album, also came in to play on a couple of tracks. I loved how casual they were, but also how excited they seemed about checking out what we were up to.

The band arrived a week or so before we started recording,

hanging out in clubs, going to watch bands. I was the only resident of the city, so I became the 'tour guide'. They were living in Oakwood Apartments on Barham Boulevard, right near Universal Studios. They had a little set-up in Mark's room so they could record ideas as they arrived. Mark was sharing with Tony, so I guess it was the party room, too.

We recorded at Danny Saber's Kevorkian's Lab on Wonderland Avenue – I would get dropped off at the apartments about noon and we would all drive over to the studio together. In the car, the music was cranked up, the roof down, the sunglasses on. Clichéd? Fucking definitely. But I love that little ritual set-up.

I like to do some kind of ritual set-up with most albums, and indeed each song, whether in the writing or the delivery of the final lead vocal. I set up the process, building myself up for the big moment. But the drive over Mulholland was particularly special. It's a mostly two-lane B-road and occasional dirt track. We would exit from the 101 South with views of the city, Los Angeles basin and San Fernando Valley, and of the Hollywood Hills and Santa Monica mountains. It gave its name to a brilliant David Lynch film that was about to come out. In the afternoon, it was a sweet-smelling miracle: eucalyptus and jasmine with an abundance of wildlife, rabbits, eagles, hawks and deer. In the evening or early hours of the morning, it was silent – apart from the occasional sound of crickets when we stopped at a red light, soulful and mysterious.

The atmosphere had everything to do with the way the songs were shaping up. We would be writing in the daytime, but then we would record in a completely blacked-out room on the third floor of Danny's house, which we started calling the junkie den. Just writing those two words sends a shiver down my spine.

Every one of us at some point or other said either we were not going to have a mad one or we weren't going to go crazy at all while we were working. But every day it got a little darker and every next day we started a little later. I was doing huge amounts of cocaine. I had a dealer with me permanently. He used to sleep on Mark's sofa and would come to meet me round at Danny's after dinner. I spent less and less time at home.

This went on for seven weeks. Initially we were conscientious and would start work at three in the afternoon, but by the end of it we were starting at four in the morning.

We were writing songs as we went along. We'd brought a few ideas from England, and we would start songs and finish ideas downstairs in Danny's kitchen, including 'And If I Fall', or 'California' as it was known at the time. I called it that just to see the look on Martin's face.

We wrote at Oakwood Apartments, and me and Mark, who had come over for a couple of weeks on his own before the rest of the band, had written some songs together at my house – 'Love is the Key', 'Right On' and 'Love to You'.

When it was just Mark and me, before the others arrived, we had spent a lot of time just talking and sightseeing, driving to the ocean, driving through the hills, going to clubs, cinemas, record shops, even the zoo: picking up vibes, letting them sink into our bones.

We would drive on the freeways, the 101, the 110 and the 10, and we would listen to the radio. The classic stations would be playing Isaac Hayes and Sly and The Family Stone. I remember a great moment, in the blazing heat, stuck in the traffic on our way out to Santa Monica, just before you get on the 110, tuning into the radio station. William Devaughn's 'Be Thankful for What You Got' came over the airwaves, and it was really a huge moment for me. We looked at each other and we both thought, Fucking hell, what a song! This is it. We had never heard it before and it felt like a gift. This was the vibe for the record we were going to make.

I fell in love with LA. It was the beginning of a love story that lasted twelve years. Maybe I am still in love with it. It's never going to go anywhere – I can always go back.

It's a city with a completely unique feeling, unlike anywhere else in the world. It's such a massive place and you can get lost in every sense. People constantly move in and people constantly ship out; it's quite a vicious city at times. But that's its appeal: like moths to a flame.

I could never have lived there without Michelle. She was my chaperone and my bodyguard! She never missed a trick.

In the twelve years that it was my home, I saw at least half a dozen bands that I knew from back in England come to LA to try and make a record, and every time they seemed to tank. They ended up leaving with varying degrees of critical and commercial flop on their hands. Either they lost it by getting too caught up in the myth or they lost it on drugs. Beware, the drugs are much stronger in LA!

Unless you have the steeliest willpower, LA is a very tough city to live in. It can suck you in and spit you out like nowhere else. But through a mixture of luck and judgement The Charlatans seemed to get it right. We even managed to make one of our finest records there.

We are truly the best band around when our backs are up against the wall. When people say, 'Oh, The Charlatans, the most cursed band in the world,' they should think of the many things we have got right: going to Los Angeles and throwing ourselves into the culture, stepping out of our comfort zone and making such a record to be proud of. That in itself, after what I have seen, is a major success.

Bands often acquire taglines which get attached by journalists every time their name crops up – the sibling rivalry behind Oasis, U2's bombast, Coldplay's beigeness, and so on. And the one that crops up with The Charlatans over and over again is that we are The Unluckiest Band in the World.

When it comes to the question of fortune, surely the unluckiest band in the world is the one you've never heard of. Maybe the guy from the label coming to check them out missed the gig from having a flat tyre on the motorway. Don't get me wrong: we have had our fair share of misfortune as well as good fortune along the way, but not such a glut of the former that the 'unlucky' tag fits. Maybe I'm just an inherently positive person, but the fact that I found the other members of the band and they found me I regard as an amazing piece of luck.

If there is an elephant in the room that needs addressing then I'm more than happy to deal with it. One of the most annoying parts of the unlucky thing relates to Rob's death. It's distasteful to attribute the death of a friend to bad luck.

Imagine the band as four members of a family, and we have endured no more or less 'bad luck' than four siblings would face in more than two decades. We're survivors who have overcome any differences we might have had, and the way we still write and perform means so much to all of us.

Our principal connection right from the start has been with the people who listen to our music. For our first few albums we would read reviews and hear directly from the fans. We always wanted to develop and keep moving forwards, and this would inevitably lead to being in vogue and sometimes out of it. But throughout all the changes there would be stories that people shared with us, stories that made it clear what the music meant to them. Over time people have been able to let us know how the band interacts with the story of their lives. These stories come from all over the world.

Recently, Mark and I toured the UK doing some reworkings of our songs with an acoustic feel, although each night we would go electric for a few songs too. The Dylanesque shouts of 'Judas' each night as I announced this never failed to make me smile. We had recorded our *Warm Sounds* EP, and it was great to be able to play small venues around the country with the stripped-down show – it wasn't The Charlatans, but it was versions of the songs we did as the band.

After one of the gigs a member of the audience stopped us and told us that it had been a watershed moment in his life. He and his wife had been to watch The Charlatans perform as a full band nineteen times. Going to see the band was their thing: always travelling together to see us, going to festivals we played. That was our only involvement in their lives. They had never spoken to us but shared special times with us. He was in his mid thirties and said that his wife had died a couple of years earlier. The devastation of the loss meant he felt he had to let the band go too. He just couldn't face it – he wouldn't be able to enjoy or even endure a gig alone.

When he heard about the acoustic gigs he told himself it was maybe something he could manage – that it would make him remember their shared times but without it being too raw. He had bought a ticket and had watched the gig. Although deeply emotional, he felt it was part of his process of coping with life ahead. To have been such a significant part of their lives without actually knowing them is an astonishing thing.

Almost every song, from the most well known to B-sides and album tracks, seems to have had a special meaning and significance for someone. Every time I hear about these connections, it amazes me. Once, an excited guy passed on his thanks for something I took little part in but he wanted to share. Ten years earlier, he had been offered a job abroad and impulsively took it. His girlfriend had commitments in the UK and he thought they would find it very hard to maintain a relationship in different countries. They parted, and he thought it would be difficult for her to move on if he stayed in touch, so reluctantly they said goodbye. Ten years later, he had a sudden realization that he'd made a terrible mistake. Their shared love of The Charlatans would be his catalyst: he bought two tickets, packed in his job and flew home. Unannounced, he went to her door a couple of days before the gig with the tickets. She was with him when we were speaking.

It sounds like something out of a romcom, but these stories need soundtracks, and it's a good feeling to provide some of them.

Having said that I do know a guy whose wife only allows him to listen to The Charlatans in the garage!

So, about that unlucky thing? I just don't get it – I sometimes feel like the luckiest person alive, but I don't often say it just in case something bad happens. I know that at certain points in life you come to a natural full stop and crave something new. Who knows what my life would have been like at 32 if I hadn't been in The Charlatans? That's how old I was when I first started going out with Michelle. We often said to each other that we would have met anyway, that it was karma, we were soul mates and we were made for each other, we were 'meant to be'. But the truth is more likely that we would never have met.

Our adventures took us everywhere: backstage at The Rolling Stones' Hollywood Bowl gig, front and centre seats for Eddie Izzard at Tiffany's. Our wedding was at Laguna Beach, with a reception at the Chateau Marmont – an occasion made even better by the fact our record company picked up the bill.

We lived in the Hollywood hills; in many ways it was the dream existence. Admittedly the showbiz and glitzy lifestyle weren't entirely me, but because Michelle liked it, I liked it. We were good together. I was a lad from Salford who'd grown up in Northwich, and she was a Georgia peach living in LA. An unscheduled visit to the Cheshire Salt Museum would be as unlikely for her as me stopping off in Little Five Points, GA. Or nipping into Hollywood, CA. But I did get to go there with the band and Michelle and I met after our gig at the John Anson Ford Amphitheater.

Aged 38 I realized I had a problem with drink and drugs. Who's to say that I wouldn't have got into that anyway living in Northwich? Though in truth this wasn't county-level addiction, this was more like Olympic drug-taking. I certainly wouldn't have had the experience and the resources to seek help unless I had been so openly surrounded by the perils and demons that inhabit rock 'n' roll souls.

I am proud to have met, talked to and been smiled at by Elliott Smith. I wouldn't have had the opportunity to make friends with, have a spat with and make up with Anton Newcombe from Brian Jonestown Massacre, a man I admire greatly but who I would definitely file under troubled genius. I certainly wouldn't have had the adventures with Alan McGee.

In 1992 I was sitting naked at the back of the bus, high on anything I could get my hands on, calling management and band meetings and keeping a straight face. I was acting like a tour bus emperor, a cocaine Caligula. If I had had pets, they would certainly have been given as senior a role as I could have invented a title for.

In 1994 I found myself at the front of the queue for singing duties with The Chemical Brothers. It was *my* phone that rang, when frankly they could have had anyone they wanted.

In 1995 I got an unexpected call from a journalist called Johnny Cigarettes saying that The Charlatans had got Single of the Week in the *NME* with 'Just When You're Thinking Things Over'. Freakily, the same week Blur and Oasis had their battle with the singles 'Country House' and 'Roll With It'.

Also in 1995 we had our second No. 1 album, and it was in some ways even sweeter this time round, like a nectarine that had gone through the rounds, been done for breach of the peace, been put in prison and come out a peach. It was sweeeet!!

In 1997 with *Tellin' Stories*, guess what? It went to No. 1.

Us and Us Only: No. 2.

Wonderland – did I say that went to No. 1 as well? If I did I lied. It went to No. 2.

I think of all the great things that have happened to me as part of this unlucky band.

Meeting and becoming friends with New Order, Paul Weller, Mick and Joe from The Clash, Johnny Marr, Madness, Mighty Boosh's Noel Fielding, Sam Morton, Joaquin Phoenix, Juliette Lewis and John McEnroe.

Being taken to see Woody Allen play clarinet in a hotel in Manhattan.

Meeting Alex Ferguson with my dad at Old Trafford.

Opening for The Rolling Stones, talking to Keith about *Pirates of the Caribbean,* having Mick tell me I could use his giant metal fans on stage as I would 'probably melt in the Bulgarian heat'.

Having Sting put his hand out to help me off stage when we opened for The Police in Europe.

Having Ronnie Wood play a trick on me and locking me in his fridge that was the size of a modest apartment.

Partying at the Playboy Mansion.

Hanging out with David Bowie in the Isle of Wight.

Becoming friends with Terry Hall, playing matchmaker and introducing him to his future wife.

Driving around LA with Dave Davies of The Kinks in his 1962 Ford Falcon.

Smoking backstage with Toots.

Being included in the Christmas celebrations and eating Christmas dinner with The Horrors.

Recording with Pip Brown, otherwise known as Ladyhawke, one of my favourite people in the world.

Now, where was I? Ah yes, making *Wonderland* . . .

Working with Danny Saber was an experience. He was talented, interesting and hard work all at the same time. He'd sprinkled his magic on everyone from Marilyn Manson to Busta Rhymes and Seal. He was a multi-instrumentalist and at one point even slyly suggested that he take over the roles of the other three members of the band. Don't get me wrong: he was only interested in making a good record, but that single-mindedness seemed to exclude some social skills – although maybe he could be considered a charmer when compared to Phil Spector, who would think nothing of pulling a gun to ensure he got the perfect take.

Every time we played in LA Danny would show up as a fan and a friend. I always loved seeing him, and Mark would end up jamming back at his studio, so it made sense for us to work together. But Danny had some of the traits of an egomaniac, and he took the view that Jon, Martin and Tony held the band back. They were all aware of this potentially unhealthy situation, but we continued talking to him in the hope he would give up on his fiendish plot of sidelining them.

I just wanted to further our horizons. Our original sound was linked to the Mad/Manchester scene. Next up came the geographically expanded Britpop. But I had always wanted to be an international band and thought that by keeping away from our comfort zone, by recording in LA and not going home to our families every night, we would keep the dynamic raw and fresh.

We had all lived close to the studio during the making of *Us and Us Only*, and I think the band spirit suffered from the burden of our outside responsibilities and our being fragmented. It was still a great record, but musically and conceptually I wanted more.

I can see why everyone was puzzled, though. With our big advance from signing to Universal, we had built our own studio space, the Big Mushroom: a rehearsal room, storage space and recording studio. We recorded all of *Us and Us Only* there, and it worked out really well. But with *Wonderland*, I, at least, wanted to keep as far away from Manchester as possible.

I'd been surrounding myself with great falsetto voices. I loved the way Kurt Wagner from Lambchop had all but ditched his deep, dark country-singing timbre for a more soulful approach on his recent album *Nixon*, and since moving to LA I had found a beaten-up copy of Curtis Mayfield's *Back to the World* in Michelle's compact collection of albums. I had been a fan of Curtis for a long time but had never really stepped outside The Impressions' first album and *Superfly*. Now I was hooked and inspired.

Danny had his girlfriend, Stacy Plunk, living with him at the time, and she had a big part to play in the record. She was a back-up singer from the South, a country girl who had sung with Jerry Lee Lewis, Willie Mitchell and Ann Peebles. Stacy was cool! She could sing gospel, blues and country, and so we got her involved from the get-go, and she became a big part of the atmosphere of the album. We would write parts for her to sing and hum backing vocals on, melodies with her in mind. It was something that we had never done before, but we got the bug and began to think about having other great musicians involved.

Twiggy 'Jeordie' Ramirez (Marilyn Manson/NIN/A Perfect Circle) would hang out at the house, as would Bernard Fowler (Rolling Stones/Herbie Hancock/Bootsy Collins), and it wasn't long before they were singing along. Both supplied backing vocals and Twiggy played additional bass on 'You're So Pretty – We're So Pretty'. (Unfortunately they didn't get credited on the album sleeve for these contributions.) Jim Keltner (check out Wikipedia – he's played with everyone!) did percussion on 'Love to You' and 'A Man Needs to Be Told', and then there was Daniel Lanois, U2's producer, playing pedal steel on 'A Man Needs to Be Told'.

Every couple of days we would have gangs of people showing up, taking a listen, wanting to party with us. It was mainly Harry the Dog and his crew. They would show up around

2 a.m., after the Cat and Fiddle pub had shut, bring over 'party supplies', have a listen and give the thumbs-up. The fact that it was a free-for-all added to the atmosphere. I love people popping in and out. It's not an office. It was a very cool place to hang out, and a great place to work in.

We weren't there for very long though. Initially, Mark and I went over to the house for a couple of days. We worked on 'Love is the Key' and recorded a demo of it to prove to the band that going to LA to work with Danny was a good idea. Altogether we had just four weeks there with all the band, writing and recording. Then there was a final week with me, Mark and Tony. The album was born!

We captured the city, the dark nights, the sunshine and crazy hours, the wildlife, a couple of fire alarms, and I think we even got the smell of cocaine, smoking and jasmine in the grooves – some potent cocktail. We were giving Sly Stone a run for his money.

I had taken to wearing flares again, shirtless and no shoes, and I had The Doors and Danny Sugarman's book *Wonderland Avenue* in my mind constantly. This was the street where legends were born, and I honestly think that with our album *Wonderland* we added to them.

We did a few overdubs at the Big Mushroom, sadly without Danny. He is not a good flyer – well, he certainly said no to economy – but we were careful not to lose what we had captured in LA. Like divorced parents we would always have joint custody of *Wonderland*.

Not everyone in the band would look back at working with Danny and say that it was a pleasant experience. At times it was really difficult. He could be an asshole. But I really liked what he did, and I think the conflicts between us added something to the music. And we all agreed it was a great album.

I don't think Danny and Tony took each other seriously,

certainly not at first. Tony had worked hard on the previous record, his debut for the band, and he felt a huge weight lift off his shoulders after its success. He felt he had proved himself, and now, quite rightly, he was feeling frisky and wanted to be even more involved.

This wasn't to Danny's liking – he only wanted to work with me and Mark. When he recorded with Black Grape, he played everything. Being a multi-instrumentalist, Danny is used to working on his own in the darkness of his upstairs recording studio, and he likes to work at his own pace and choose his own hours. He really can play everything! He is fast; he can mix; he can do everything except sing and dance. Maybe he can even do that, I don't know.

Eventually he began to respect Tony when he realized that he had come up with most of the musical ideas for 'Is It In You' and 'You're So Pretty'.

Danny would provide beats for Mark and me to sing and play to. He wanted to play bass, or he would get Twiggy in to play bass, and then he would get Stacy to do the backing vocals. He has a vision, and he has a sound. The thing about Danny is that he lives in his studio in LA and rarely goes out. He orders food in, and would occasionally ask Martin or Jon to go and get him a pizza.

If we had been producing *Wonderland* ourselves we would have unconsciously filled the record up with frills – just because that's what naturally happens when five members of the band are producing a record. Making something via a committee is never the best solution, and Danny worked as a dictator, even going so far as to wear an SS outfit on occasions (particularly unsettling given that Danny is Jewish). The record needed him.

'A Man Needs to Be Told' is probably the centrepiece and, for me, the most interesting song on the album. It completely divided our audience. The song was written as a response to the music scene becoming macho again. I was quite despondent about it. When the Haçienda kicked off in 1987–8, I witnessed grown men from the building sites dancing on the stage, hugging each other. I thought I was witnessing a breakthrough. I didn't have to walk around with clenched fists any more. You had to do that in Manchester in the early '80s. In the underground market, and the Arndale Centre especially, there was always a chance you would inconveniently get beaten up.

But then, with the rise of lad culture, through Britpop and beyond, this beautiful moment seemed like it had never happened. Now I wanted to write something fragile, something without ego, almost feminine, as a protest. And to disassociate myself from that scene.

Danny really was an odd one. The band would often catch him doing my drugs behind my back. Sometimes even on camera. But having said that, a fellow drug-user nicking coke is often viewed as playing the game.

He became more and more demanding as the sessions went on, over money mostly. He knew that we were only there for a limited amount of time, but if he didn't get what he was due, the shutters came down and the drawbridge came up. There was somebody home but the lights weren't on.

Deep down, I knew Danny would never come to the Big Mushroom to mix *Wonderland*. He promised, and we were all prepared to be accommodating, but things were difficult. Eventually we came to the conclusion that Danny couldn't function outside Los Angeles. Many people can't. I can understand why. The city is beautiful. Everything you could ever want is there, and more. So he wanted to mix it in LA? Who wouldn't?

For *Us and Us Only* we'd had Rob Schnapf and Tom Rothrock (Beck/Elliott Smith) come over to do some mixes. We couldn't get them studio time in Abbey Road, but they wanted the Abbey Road mixing desk, so we found them a place with the same equipment in Rochdale – not quite St John's Wood, but, hey! Never mind. Martin in particular felt let down by Danny's failure to come over and do the mixing on *Wonderland*. We ended up mixing it with Jim Spencer, which was great, but with Danny gone, some of the space began to get filled up. It was perhaps more polished in the end than it would have been if Danny had mixed it. He would have kept it completely stripped down. Still, when Jim and I mixed 'You're So Pretty', I was thinking this is as good as New Order's 'Confusion', and I knew that it had to be the opening song on the album.

★ ★ ★

So there we were with this great album. We were all geared up to do well with it. We had label support in LA, and we did an eight-date tour, with Black Rebel Motorcycle Club supporting us, in the summer as a taster for what was to come. We were ready to go with our autumn tour.

We released in the US on 11 September 2001.

The autumn tour was cancelled.

8. HOLLYWOOD

Writing a book is a strange activity. People know me for writing lyrics, but that's a different thing altogether. Lyrics reveal feelings and parts of your character in short bursts. They offer a glimpse of someone, catching a part of their personality but in a light of their own choosing. Writing a book is much more revealing, like having an arc light shone on you for a prolonged period. At first you can do nothing but blink at the glare.

Even the word 'autobiography' sounds a little too grand – to me it suggests a book about Winston Churchill, say, or Errol Flynn. Autobiography has partly been devalued now, with glamour models chucking out a volume just in time for Christmas, and footballers, barely out of their teens, doing their urban philosophizing (in the words of their ghostwriter, of course).

I grew up in the 1970s and 1980s, so I'm inclined to view my past in terms of TV and film – *Kes* and *Stand By Me* perfectly capture my early youth, where responsibilities were absent but every day was a morality minefield and a series of massive lessons in social standing. At other times my life has seemed like anything from *GoodFellas* to *Twin Peaks*. But throughout it all I've retained a strong sense of my self. Maybe at times I seemed just round the corner from death or just over the road from utter madness – but at the time it felt like what I should be doing.

When I was growing up, Hollywood might as well have been on another planet, and the music business was some kind of holy grail for any kid looking for excitement. I never dreamed I'd end up in either, let alone both. But I did, and I was no better prepared for any of it than you are right now or than anyone else would be for that matter.

Everyone has a view on Hollywood from a distance, ranging from 'It's where all the beautiful people go' to 'It's full of dickheads' – after spending twelve years there my conclusion is somewhere between the two. Both opinions are right.

Like a lot of people of my generation I got my first taste of Hollywood through classics like *Superman*, *Jaws* and *Grease* – in my case at the Regal Cinema in Northwich. As I got older I went with mates to watch films like *The Blues Brothers* and John Carpenter's *The Thing*. Then there were first dates, watching John Hughes's teen masterpieces *Sixteen Candles* and *Pretty in Pink*.

Then videos appeared on the scene. A kid down the street had a Betamax system, and we would watch horror movies and video nasties – *Friday the 13th*, *Last House on the Left*, *I Spit on Your Grave*, *The Exorcist* – as well as the occasional soft-porn tape from a mate's father's stash. Not that they were porno by today's standards. Films like *Electric Blue* look more like a Strokes video than triple-X action. Still, they were enough to keep five teenagers in wide-eyed awe.

I remember what a stir films like *The Warriors* and *The Wanderers* caused and how much controversy they kicked up. They were apparently corrupting the youth and knocking the world off its axis, which of course made me want to watch them even more. At this time I was going to the local Northwich disco dressed in my Crombie with the words 'Police killed Liddle Towers' emblazoned on it. The disco was run by the local police.

One day, without discussion, my dad threw the Crombie in the bin. My mum pointed out sympathetically that I didn't need to work hard to draw attention to myself. 'People notice you enough anyway,' she said. I knew what she was getting at . . . but it definitely still didn't feel enough!

I got a clip round the ear from my dad for getting my ear pierced, the newly punctured lobe making the clip twice as painful. But parental involvement in my sartorial journey was not always negative. I tried not to advertise the fact, but my favourite bondage trousers ever were made by my mum, out of a pair of cricket trousers. I had stopped playing and become a punk, and my mum's involvement with my punk odyssey was probably based on her disapproval of waste rather than her hatred of society or her allegiance to the spirit of '77. Anyway, the trousers were literally the talk of the town.

My ambition at this time was to be Damien from *The Omen*. I wanted to wake up with 666 on my head. This may sound ridiculous, but I identified with the combination of his neat, unassuming appearance and his dark demeanour: angelic features, but turn your back and you would have a pole through the top of your head. Later on I would identify with the Perry boys, their smart look disguising their menacing ways.

My first introduction to art-house cinema came in the '80s and early '90s, with David Lynch's *Blue Velvet*, Peter Greenaway's *The Cook, the Thief, His Wife and Her Lover*, *The Unbearable Lightness of Being*, *Betty Blue*, *Wings of Desire* and similar films. I remember sitting in the Gate Cinema in Notting Hill watching *A Short Film about Killing*, *Monsieur Hire*, *The Hairdresser's Husband* and *The Big Blue*. I feel as though it was a golden age for this type of film. Or does everyone just think that their early twenties were a special time?

Hollywood is so startlingly bright. Even the coyotes wear shades. The trees, the beach and the sky come together with the jasmine and the ocean to provide a scented, sensual soundtrack to the laid-back slacker cool. Unsurprisingly, it quickly seduced me. It was the furthest thing away from a regular life on earth that I could think of.

I never imagined that I would ever live there. In fact, I didn't even like it when I first visited in 1990, although I did like the sunshine, the surf and the boogie boards. But at the time I had a bee in my bonnet about New York being my kinda town. But I grew to love LA, and through a strange series of events I ended up living there in the beautiful hills, right opposite the famous sign, the most recognized placename in the world.

My first actual dealings with Hollywood came about when we were recording our first album, *Some Friendly*, in Wrexham in the summer of 1990. We had a song called '109 Part 2', which included dialogue from the Alan Parker film *Angel Heart*. Robert De Niro played the part of Louis Cypher, a mysterious boiled-egg-eating client of Mickey Rourke's gumshoe, Harry Angel. I sampled De Niro's line 'Some religions think that the egg is the symbol of the soul, did you know that?'

Rourke replies, 'No, I didn't know that.'

'Would you like an egg?' says De Niro.

I was told that to get clearance I would have to write directly to De Niro. So in my neatest handwriting I wrote:

Dear Mr De Niro,

My name is Tim Burgess, I am in an up and coming UK band called The Charlatans and we are at this moment recording our debut album.

We are all big fans of your film *Angel Heart* and your character Louis Cypher.

We have a song called '109 Part 2', where we have sampled your voice, and I am writing to tell you in hope that you would give me and the band permission to use some of the dialogue.

I have included two versions of the song, one with you on, and one with you off. I think you will agree that the one with you on is the best.

Really hope you say yes.
Sincerely, Tim

It was a handwritten letter with a Wrexham postmark, and before we'd finished the album we had got a reply. Not only did he say yes, he said he loved it!

I suppose this was when I first thought that Hollywood stars might be accessible.

Eva Mendes is a fan of The Charlatans, as is Chloë Sevigny. Of course, I am only going to tell you about the famous ones! There's no accounting for taste, and there's no predicting where your fans will come from.

In my dreams, the only three people from the Hollywood and film world I ever really wanted to care about The Charlatans or be somehow interested in them were Samantha Morton, Joaquin Phoenix and David Lynch.

I first came across Sam Morton in the television series *Band of*

Gold, in which she played a prostitute called Tracey. I watched it avidly each Sunday night, altering my recording schedules to make sure I was in front of a TV. Around the same time she appeared as a pregnant girl in *Cracker*. The first time I saw her in a film at the cinema was in *Sweet and Lowdown*, for which she received an Oscar nomination. She played a mute girl alongside Sean Penn, with Woody Allen directing.

I met Sam for the first time at the Isle of Wight in June 2009. I always hoped she would come along to a gig. I had never met her but I had seen her in The Horrors' video for 'Sheena is a Parasite', directed by Chris Cunningham, so I knew we shared a taste for great music. I couldn't have been more pleased to see her walk out of the crowd in the venue that I was curating that day. It was a 10,000-capacity big-top tent, where she had been watching the likes of The Black Lips, The Pains of Being Pure at Heart and The Horrors, with us playing at the end. She seemed as happy to see me as I was to see her. In fact, she had recently been in touch asking for permission to use one of our songs for her directorial debut. It reminded me of our brush with De Niro, so I happily gave her clearance, knowing I would be proud of the results. We've kept in touch ever since.

I first became aware of Joaquin Phoenix when I heard the harrowing 911 call that was played all over the world after his brother's death outside the Viper Room in 1993. Joaquin was just 19 years old at the time. My first sighting was watching him being seduced by Nicole Kidman in the Gus van Sant film *To Die For*.

In Los Angeles in 2007 I ended up spending three weeks in a studio on the corner of Beverley and Fairfax with Joaquin and Antony Langdon. From what I could gather the music was mostly being written by Conceptualized, and was paid for by Joaquin, though it was certainly Antony's record. The project name was 'Victoria', and I was attending the sessions with Alan McGee. According to McGee we were there as tastemakers . . .

Joaquin's intensity in the studio was every bit as captivating as his performance as Johnny Cash in *Walk the Line* – from clearing the room of studio executives and hapless agents without warning, to smashing his head through a plate-glass window in what seemed to be a show of just how extreme he could be. I didn't want to win that game, or even join in.

But along with this went his impeccable attention to detail. It was hugely inspiring.

'Victoria', Take One

The project was meticulously produced by Joaquin, with Antony's Bowie-inspired, grandiose, Anthony Newley-styled English warblings and Joaquin's words about demons, secrets and the past, with occasional guitar by Casey Affleck thrown into the mix, and me doing backing vocals and harmonies. I never spent studio time with Phil Spector, Brian Wilson or Charles Manson, but at times it seemed like all three were in the room. I wouldn't have missed it for the world.

'Victoria', Take Two

'Victoria', Take One, was scrapped for no obvious reason, so I concluded that the contributions of myself and Alan McGee were no longer required. Some tastemakers we had turned out to be!

Alan was already moving on. He'd met Lisa Marie Presley at a dinner held at Joaquin's house and wanted her to make a country album or a covers album – I can't remember which, and I'm not sure if it ever saw the light of day either.

Joaquin looked like he lived in a car, and his car looked like someone lived in it! He would drive me the thirty minutes home each night, and it was on these journeys that I actually got a real feel for him. He would tell me stories about his films with the same gusto you might use to tell a story of a recent trip to the post office. I loved him even more for this, because he was one of Hollywood's most famous faces.

He would say things to me like, 'I learned to play the guitar for a movie that I was in,' or 'There was this film I was in where I had to wear, like, some robes and a laurel crown.' I worked out that these cryptic statements were references to *Walk the Line* and *Gladiator*, two of the biggest award-winning movies of the last decade. He was intriguing and humble, crazy but always generous. He threw his car keys to me across a parking lot one night, saying, 'You can keep hold of this for as long as you like.' It was a blacked-out 4 × 4 BMW. I knew he meant it, though I didn't accept. How could I? I would have missed out on our little evening road trips.

He could move around undercover pretty well, wearing understated clothes. His general demeanour wasn't that of a movie star. As McGee put it, he was more 'bag man'. We would always go to the back entrance of a club for discretion's sake, and always entourage-free – unless you count Antony, me and McGee as entourage. A Hollywood A-lister, a legendary Scottish music mogul, one of the UK's foremost ex-pat musical talents . . . and me.

Once, when asked by a doorman, 'Who the fuck are you?', Joaquin looked uncomfortable and started to bumble around, saying under his breath, 'Dude, don't do this.' I knew him by now, and I knew he wasn't enjoying what was happening. He leaned in close to the guy's ear, glanced around a little, jacket sleeve over hand, over mouth. He whispered to the doorman. He either said his name or issued the scariest and shortest threat known to man, as immediately the entire security team jumped into action, parted like the Red Sea and led us to a table – the kind of table that you would imagine was permanently reserved for the imminent arrival of some local mafia don.

'Victoria', Take Three

Having been told that my vocals and contributions had been stripped from the 'Victoria' record, I found out through a friend of a friend that my voice was back on. Things had very quickly moved forwards and sideways.

My voice was now being included, supposedly, on Joaquin's latest recordings – a hip-hop project. It was much reported, very much mocked, and perhaps eternally destined to be a 'hotly anticipated' record. At this moment the release date is still unconfirmed.

★ ★ ★

I met Michael Douglas at a Paul Weller gig, of all places. I say of all places, but then I remember hearing that Catherine Zeta Jones was a big fan of The Style Council. Michelle, in a stage whisper, pointed out that CZJ, who was giddily running around, chatting and working the crowd like minor European royalty, was rocking a lot of jewellery. She was over-accessorized, over-excited and over in Hollywood.

I used to love these nights, so much fun, a Northwich punk standing next to a Welsh girl who had done well and was re-acquainting herself with the music of her youth, made by her hero.

Anyway, Michelle grabbed Michael and told him I was in a band called The Charlatans and was going to be playing the

El Ray Theater on Wilshire Boulevard. Michael seemed interested, but looking back I think it was more to do with the venue
than my impending gig. In fact I am sure that was the case as he
gave me a near-perfect history of the place. I think he took my
open-mouthed stare as a green light to continue with his ora-
tion, but it was more to do with the fact I was getting a virtual
architectural tour from Gordon Gekko himself. 'Only in LA' is
the expression that definitely applies here.

I mentioned to Michael that I really loved his film *The Game*.
He nodded and smiled. I happened to mention that I knew an
actor who had appeared in it, a Scottish friend of mine that I had
not seen for a few months, whose favourite song of ours was
'My Beautiful Friend'.

'You mean the dude with the scars on his face?' said Michael,
marking out an extended smile-shape with his finger. 'I hear
it's referred to as a "Glasgow smile"!' We were talking about
Tommy Flanagan, a Glaswegian who had come over to LA and
had landed parts in *Gladiator* and *Braveheart*. I met him when
I had been in LA for three months. We hit it off after he bowled
up to me outside Barney's Beanery, a rock 'n' roll haunt of some
repute, and started enthusing about a Charlatans performance
on Jools Holland's *Later* show. We had mutual friends who
would invite us to parties, and we definitely shared the same
glint in our eye that only someone who knows, knows.

Much later Tommy was involved in an incident at his place
near Lanewood, where we ended up after a party one night, that
helped turn me against the city. The apartment backed onto the
Hollywood High School, where every weekend they had band
practice. It was beautiful and innocent enough, but if you had a
hangover it could be extremely annoying. The perky football
kids and brass-band boffins were the polar opposite of the
whacked-out freaks who circled the flat in search of their lost
sunglasses and more of what they'd had the night before. It was

a scene of post-party carnage that would be played out every weekend to the point of tedium: usually the same characters, sometimes with a gatecrasher or two.

This particular day sticks in my mind because it took a swerve from the norm. It was 7 a.m. and a fight broke out between Tommy and some other party animal. Tommy had a dog, a boxer called Papillon, which was a canine version of him, excitable and always on high alert. As the fight continued the dog took a perch on the back rest of an armchair and started barking in time with the blows.

His owner had blood all over his face and had had his two front teeth kicked out. Tommy was scrabbling around on the floor, still with shades on, trying to find his missing incisors. He looked like Gary Oldman in *True Romance* without the dreads, and coincidentally it was Oldman's dentist who would later fix the teeth.

That could only happen if he found them, though, and his bloodied features, sunglasses and manic dog weren't helping. The fighting eventually stopped and the dog joined in the search, while the Hollywood High marching band kept on playing and the school football team began to practise in the background. It was like *The Warriors* meets the video for *Tusk* by Fleetwood Mac. I began to feel like an autistic kid who's unable to cope with the sensory overload.

Harry the Dog said it was the worst violence he had ever seen in LA, but this kind of incident was becoming a regular part of my life, the fallout from a house full of borderline loons. I was moving gradually towards the decision that it had to come to an end, though it took me another eighteen months to act on it.

9. GETTING STRAIGHT

Whenever I was away from America, I missed the strong and sweet Hollywood cocaine that I'd grown accustomed to. It had been through a limited number of hands since its journey began in Colombia and had less of the teething powder, animal wormer or baking soda that routinely gets added by each new vendor to keep margins up. Like some people can spot a good wine, I had become a connoisseur of the devil's dandruff.

I don't want to glorify my use of drugs, and I am acutely

aware of the methods drug cartels use which heap misery on huge areas of South America. But these are never your concerns when you're lost in the middle of it all. You have a clearer view of things after you stop, and a level of honesty can be brought in that is not possible while you are still an addict. So what I'm saying is that anyone who might be shocked or upset by this – hi Mum, hi Dad – can be happy in the knowledge that it is in the past, and this candid talk isn't available to anyone still in the grip of drug-use. There is a level of denial that disappears when you really are done with it.

There was such a difference in quality that I used to supply to a guy in Europe – that guy was me, when I made my trips home. I was a kind of drug dealer to myself, which at least meant there was a degree of trust involved. Having said that, I'd always nick a bit just before I posted it, thinking I'd not notice when I got it in Europe. Frank Zappa has a song called 'Cocaine Decisions'. These were my cocaine decisions.

If I didn't send some into the future for me to pick up when I caught up with myself, I would spend three days running around looking for what would inevitably be the worst gear in London or Manchester. Dealers are good to those who are good to them, but non-regulars get a raw deal.

Sending it in records was always my modus operandi, and always in a record by a band whose records I would never actually buy. I don't know why, but I imagined that my case would be thrown out after it had dawned on the wily magistrate that I couldn't possibly own a Jamiroquai record. Cocaine decisions.

Transporting the stuff took many forms. On tour buses I'd be travelling over the borders with my stash in a rucksack tied to a spare Leslie speaker horn parked at the very back in a flight case under the Hammond. It worked pretty well. I doubted that even the most chirpy pup would be nimble enough to clamber all the way back there through that – squeezing among the gear looking for the other gear.

Or I would put a bag of charity shop clothes and a consignment of pills anonymously in the hold of a National Express bus travelling to Europe, then catch a plane and meet the bus at its final destination. How do you do? Yes, thank you very much!

My DJ box was a flight case with approximately fifty records tightly packed in it – a perfect opportunity for taping a gram to the inside of the sleeves for a treat when the records were played later in the evening. The one-in-a-million chance of the drugs being found by someone else was reassuring, yet the Russian-roulette feel of the whole thing made the already enjoyable DJ jobs that little bit better.

It became a slight obsession, and on one trip to the UK I became stressed when I realized I'd forgotten to post anything to my destination. So I packed me an eight-ball (3.5 grams) in my belongings. When I arrived in London, I got a call to say my bag hadn't made it and would be on the next flight; they would deliver to my hotel within 24 hours.

My jangling nerves and paranoia, mixed with one too many films, led me to envisage half a dozen plain-clothed officers standing around my suitcase, laid open on a table in an interview room at Paddington Green police station. Underwear is held in tweezers at arm's length. Socks are in a see-through plastic bag marked exhibit A.

It was a very long 24 hours. Not only was I without my drugs, but I was looking at a 3 stretch. I didn't even know what a 3 stretch was but I'd heard it somewhere.

At last there was a knock on my hotel-room door. 'Mr Burgess, your luggage.'

I opened the door and there he stood – holding my bag was the least convincing undercover cop I'd ever seen. He paused and said, 'You'll be in a right state without this,' evidently a knowing reference to the drugs. I looked up and down the corridor, as he surely had some sort of back-up. But there was no one. I looked at him and he gestured towards me again with my case. He was frowning and wondering why I hadn't taken it. I took it. He asked me to sign his docket and he was off.

I was a free man, and I was pretty excited. There was only one way to celebrate. But I castigated myself for my stupidity and vowed I'd never do it again.

Like any drug-user I usually failed to include the consequences in my list of concerns. A conviction in the UK or US would have made travel and visas a logistical nightmare for the band.

That was my life in The Charlatans for about three years. During the period of *Up at the Lake* and *Simpatico* I was beyond help. If anyone did try to help, I would be belligerent or I would just ignore them. No one was getting through. The real root of the problem was that I wanted to sabotage everything. At this time I wanted to destroy the band I loved because I couldn't work with our manager, Steve Harrison. I couldn't understand why the rest of the band wanted to keep hold of him when a clean severance would have been much more dignified.

Would it have saved me from my self-medicating nightmare? Perhaps. Well, I have to blame something. Cocaine decisions again.

I am pretty sure that Steve was aware that relationships were at an all-time low, but he must have been at best confused and at worst living in a nightmare of uncertainty and frustration. As a band I don't think we could have been any crueller.

None of us was brave enough to face up to him and say it's over. Martin was afraid of jumping out of the frying pan into the fire, and none of us could pretend that we knew what to do. I blame myself. I was the de facto leader but too out of it to be in charge. It was a case of the one-eyed man in the kingdom of the blind.

And the rest of the band were in denial because they didn't want to admit that I was the leader.

I didn't give a fuck. They didn't see it because he had been there from the start, but I'd lost all confidence in him. In fact I no longer had a relationship with him. He was good in the beginning, granted. But the band had made it easy for him. *We* were good. We were fresh.

There were situations in which he pretended he knew how to do something just because he was too proud to say he didn't know what he was doing. It's one of my least favourite traits. True, I don't know what I am doing half the time. I don't think in itself that's a bad thing, in fact you can stumble upon great things sometimes that way, but I do think it's important to let people know when you don't know what you're doing.

In many circumstances it could be a dangerous thing, and Steve just flunked his way through. And when he messed up, the repercussions always fell on the band. He just wasn't strong enough defending us or fighting our corner. He often told us that Peter Grant was his hero, but Peter Grant would have taken a bullet for Led Zeppelin, whereas I reckon at this stage Steve would have sold us down the river for a prawn sandwich (his favourite). In my opinion, he was out of his depth in every area, and on top of it all he was desperate for financial security, as he was facing bankruptcy. The biggest crime of all: the desperate manager of a rock 'n' roll band.

★ ★ ★

We'd all been dealt a huge blow when our accountant, Trevor Williams, a 48-year-old local who we'd completely trusted, ran off with £300,000 of the band's money. Even worse, he hadn't accounted for any of our taxes in the past five or six years and we were incurring daily penalties from the Inland Revenue – we eventually had to pay back £1.9 million.

On his court appearance in April 1999 he admitted taking our money and asked for twenty-one other cases to be taken into account. So I suppose at least we could take some solace from the fact that it wasn't anything personal. His secretary told us that he left big cheques made out to himself lying around the office, as though he wanted to be caught. I think he must have had some kind of breakdown at the end.

When we first heard that something was up, we had a crisis meeting with Steve, who told us that Williams wanted to talk to us in his house – which was, inconveniently, right opposite our newly converted studio. So I went along with Martin, Steve and our lawyer. We were curious about his motives and his methods. At the time I didn't realize the magnitude of what he'd done, and I was all ready to accept a cup of tea when we arrived, but Martin had the right approach – he had to restrain himself from punching him. Martin took it really personally. The beating never happened, but I think he did get to spit on Williams later on outside court.

Our lawyer asked him straight out why he had done it, to which he responded, 'I don't know.' And that was the only information we got out of him. Though he did say that if we didn't report him he'd do our taxes for free for the rest of his life! He ended up serving five years in prison.

And Steve? What had Steve been doing during this time? During the giddy heights of the second bout of Charlatans success, between 1995 and 1997, he had managed to build his empire up to six record shops in the northwest. I guess he took his eye off the ball while Williams (a family friend of his – he did Steve's dad's taxes) destroyed the band financially. It would take us ten years to get over it. If we ever have.

Subsequently, Steve had to declare himself bankrupt as a trader over the accountancy fiasco. A shopkeeper with no shops. He lost everything except his income as manager of The Charlatans.

So the root of all my problems were my manager and the death of Rob, and they were amplified by my increasing reliance on drugs. In the beginning, we were all so close. I loved Steve. Maybe I did rely on him too much, but I had a lot to deal with. I went from a small rehearsal room in Wednesbury to having all these hits and travelling all over the place. I remember doing press in Amsterdam at the American Hotel in 1990. Marianne Faithfull came and sat at my table and just stared at me with a sexy smile as I was doing my interview. I had a feeling that Marianne wanted me as her next love experiment! I think she was still living on the streets at the time, or maybe it was just after that period, but she was looking good!

And then on one occasion in 1993 I was backstage at the Limelight Club in New York, lying on the floor, on my back, with a girl lying next to me, on E, when Madonna walked in, shades on and her hands covering her eyes. There'd been a strong rumour before we played that she was coming to see us, and later I heard she danced all the way through the set. I wasn't surprised. The band were hot, and the Manchester scene was a worldwide phenomenon. After all, Mick Jagger had shown up in Atlanta.

Perhaps it was the deli tray, the cigarette butts and the cans of beer on the floor that caused Madonna's reaction. 'Gross!' I think she said. Or maybe, 'Oh, gross!' Anyway, she wasn't impressed. It obviously wasn't the face-to-face meeting she or, for that matter, I had hoped for.

I was beginning to get really well known. Everywhere I went, people would want me to stop and talk to them. Kids would follow me everywhere. It was fun, but I couldn't really go out any more. I was followed and photographed everywhere I went. Beggars Banquet licensed our records out in each country in the world, and in every posh office there would be an older woman, the Vice President of the label, say, who acted like she wanted me to seduce her. And I just couldn't do it. I just seemed to be running away from older women all the time. It was of course something that would have really appealed to the teenage me – maybe it was a case of being careful what you wish for.

I wanted to sort myself out; I didn't want to do rehab. So I pretty much locked myself in a room at the K West Hotel for nine days before going on tour to promote the 2006 album *Simpatico*. The first four days were awful: goose bumps, hot and cold sweats, headaches, feeling sick, wild mood swings, confusion and regret. I really wanted to do it without Michelle being around, because I knew I would take out my frustration on her. I didn't want her to see me in this state either.

I tried to take my mind off the withdrawals, but everything just seemed so dull. All the programmes on TV were mind-numbingly boring. I tried to sleep, but I could only do it sporadically. I would pace around at four in the morning. I was hot and I was cold. I wasn't aching, but my mind was craving.

Later I went to see Dr Nish Joshi, a medical guru, Princess Diana's nutritionist and an all-round health miracle worker, in Harley Street, London. After a consultation and full confession, he put me on a 21-day detox programme. I was persuaded to go by our tour manager, Curly Jobson, the brother of Richard Jobson from The Skids. 'Persuaded' isn't quite the right word – he just asked me if I wanted to go and see Nish. There was no pressure, but he was a patient and came to me with glowing reviews of the doctor. He had an appointment on Monday, the next afternoon, and invited me along. It was the best thing I could have done.

From the moment of my confession I began to feel better. I'd finally told someone about my problems. Obviously, I did have issues, but until this point I hadn't admitted them to myself. The simplicity of what I had to do hit me there and then. I had no guilt and no apologies to make.

But I was now 38, I would be 40 in a couple of years, and

I was tired of being 'That Tim', the one captured in this interview by Sylvia Patterson for *Sky* in December 1995.

Tim Burgess, singer with The Charlatans, is one of the most
likable rock stars in action.

His passion for music is inexhaustible, he dances constantly
to his own inner tune, clicking his fingers, grinning till you
think his face will split, extolling the joys of music and most
other things in life. I once danced with him in his own living
room to his own record after a deliriously drunken night out,
and left at eight in the morning, glad to find a rock singer who
didn't care two monkeys for cool.

*Here Sylvia Patterson takes him out for lunch, watches him get heroically
drunk, graciously accepts his gift of a watch, and tries to deposit him home
despite him not having a clue where he lives.*

'Mam? Your friend. He has fallen down the stairs.'

The barman is concerned. He has the look on his face of
someone who is considering calling an ambulance. Tim Burgess
is not concerned. He has the look on his face of blithe oblivion
because he, unlike the barman, is the happiest man in the world.

He is also the drunkest man in the world. And, in the last two
hours, he has not only fallen all the way down the pub stairs and
gained a profound limp, but proved himself a spectacularly
bizarre, bona fide nutter of pop rivalled only by the king of
errant lunacy himself, i.e. Bez from Black Grape.

Firstly, Tim was 'jet-lagged out of me head' so there was only
one thing for it: four bottles of wine with the Italian meal. The
Italian meal of broccoli pasta which he half ate and then enquired
four times as to whether we'd eaten yet or not. He didn't remember drinking his beer either. Waited for the return of his credit
card when it was sitting in front of him inside the leather receipt
book for half an hour. Gave me his watch, a fake $35 Rolex affair

with special countdown effect for deep-sea divers, for no reason, howling 'Cheers! Nice one! This year's been the year of presents!' Attacked the ivories of the restaurant piano player on the way out the door. Couldn't find the pub he's been drinking in for years. Started cuddling everyone; great big bear-hug embraces to knock the wind out of a typhoon. Showed everyone his new tattoo of a sleeping cartoon tiger on his back. Ended up with his head in the lap of your reporter's chum after giving her his plastic Beatles bag and all its worldly contents. Sang Oasis's 'Champagne Supernova' from the bonnet of a car. Couldn't even remember he lived in London. Was told by a homeless person in a doorway that if he didn't get up off the Soho pavement he wouldn't get a taxi to take him anywhere. He steadied himself on a wall.

'You live in Chalk Farm, Tim,' said my chum, who was the only person not on the pavement in Soho, to which he replied 'That's it! Ace! I'm going home!' So, finally, he went home, unconscious in a taxi. Or woke up in hospital, or in the wrong continent, whichever came first. For a man whose behaviour borders on the suicidal, Timothy Burgess, the people's friend, is what you'd call a life enthusiast.

He is also mad. It's a much abused word, mad, attributed to anyone with a semblance of personality, but he really is proper coo-ee clouds pan-dimensional mad mad. He doesn't sit, he grooves in his seat, shoulders undulating to some constant inner rhythm, fingers clicking, his arm shooting into the air every three seconds with mad-for-it delight. He does this in front of the waiter and the startled fellow flinches as if the Northern loon was about to sock him in the jaw for not pouring the wine fast enough.

He speaks to you on the end of your nose in a low Northern slur of pronounced inarticulacy, ending a theory with 'You know what I mean, though . . . or whatever . . .' veering into a polar opposite subject and/or emotion until you haven't a bloody clue what he's on about any more. He means everything he says. And then he says 'Fuck it!' or 'I can't be arsed!' and breaks out in uncontrollable cackles. He is a 7-year-old boy tumbling around in the deceptively big-boned body of a 27-year-old man. And a top geezer, a real-deal pop persona and the happiest man in the entire world in the zenith of a personal vindication because up until this year, he and his band were universally presumed to be, as Tim would have it, 'a gonner'.

It is the triumphant pop year of 1995. The Charlatans' triumph shone the brightest because everyone thought they were dead. From the bench on the side of Britpop pitch hysteria, they quietly brought us their fourth LP, *The Charlatans*, and from oblivion, it went straight into the charts at number one; a huge, sumptuous, celebratory album of power-pop excellence hailed as the second LP The Stone Roses took five years not to come up with.

For the second time in their six-year history, The Charlatans were number one LP titans of pop; it happened before with their debut *Some Friendly* in 1990: The Year of Baggy. Their year of *Smash Hits* superstardom, of being lost in American deserts, of psychedelic rock 'n' roll jubilation. And then The Curse began. Madchester was stoned to death in the grunge avalanche. Their new tunes were panned. Martin (Blunt – bass) went down with clinical depression. Jon (Baker – guitar) left. Mark (Collins – guitar) joined and became an alcoholic within six months. On 3 December 1992 Rob Collins (keyboards) drove the getaway car in an armed off-licence robbery. The band carried on, didn't really think he'd go to jail for, you know, real. Rob's case came to trial in September 1993; he was sentenced to eight months in Shrewsbury prison. Now, two years later, The Charlatans are enjoying a return to 'Flavour of the moment' status with, it has to be said, unfeasible gusto.

So. What went right?

'All right,' says Tim, downing at least half a pint in approximately four seconds, 'it was the realization, when Rob went to prison, of everything that we could lose. So me and Mark started to write tunes.'

It was the first time they'd written together, just the two of them. They wrote somewhere in the region of five songs every week, no matter if they were rubbish or not. They weren't and it saved their lives. And saved Tim from the demons of his inner asylum.

'I went through a real self-loathing period, me,' he says, puffing on the hour's 87th cigarette. 'Seriously. Honestly. I just hated everything that I did. When the second LP got trashed I really thought it was all my fault and everything that I ever did was shit. But there was something weird inside me that made me want to do it even more. I never did this to start with for any other reason than to be a great band. I didn't do it for the girls – I never had a real phobia about being an ugly git, I never had Pete Townshend syndrome, know what I'm saying? I just got addicted to doing LPs, which sounds really shit but it's true. So it wasn't a case of holding onto the reins; it was a case of setting them on fire and that's what we did, so . . . cheers!'

Tim didn't visit Rob in jail once.

'No,' says Tim looking suddenly forlorn, 'I apologized to him at the time but I didn't approve. Of what he'd done. Because he put my life in jeopardy and I wasn't asking for it. But we survived and I love him; he's spooky but he's a good guy at the end of the day.'

Do you know why he did it?

'For the buzz,' says Tim plainly. 'He's into danger, he's just like that' (begins fiddling with a watch which is too big even for his enormous wrists). 'I'm going to find the perfect person to give this watch to – I love giving me stuff away . . .'

How come you've never lost the plot like some of the others did?

'Dunno,' grins Tim. 'I just have a good time, me – you've just got to be yourself, haven't you? Oh God (sets his hand on fire with his fag), now I've burnt meself. I reckon I'm the *Observer* and everyone else is the *Sunday Times*, know what I'm saying?'

Frankly no.

'Rob's definitely the *Sunday Times*, he's always getting out of his mind. Rob's the kind that'll kick the door off its fookin' hinges and sleep in the bath. Oh God, I can't be doing with all this me representing the band any more! What's that there? Is it vodka?'

It's water. Maybe you should have a small sip?

'Where's me beer? Oh, I've drunk it.'

In 1983, aged 15, Tim left school with one O-level in English and a head full of Milky Way, quite possibly.

'When I left school I was told I was never gonna get a job,' he says, rolling around in his seat. 'I was fookin' told it. And it wasn't a put-down; it was just the truth – there was no opportunities in this country.'

From the age of 11 Tim had been a music obsessive. Went to see Killing Joke aged 11 in his school uniform. Spent nights hiding in his room listening to John Peel and making up imaginary set-lists for The Fall and New Order. So, naturally, his personal pop dream began.

'No,' corrects Tim breezily, 'the band thing never came into me head at all. I didn't think about anything. I thought I'd just do nothing. Did not know nothing, honestly. Then I got a job at 16, which me dad put me up for at ICI (where his father worked along with the entire population of Northwich), and everyone thought it was me dad that got me the job but it wasn't. I just said the right things. Said it was a brilliant job, said it'd be top and I could do it better than anybody else. So put your faith in me.'

And you were completely lying through your teeth?

'Honestly, between you and me,' says Tim, because he is

nuts, 'I've wanted to do every single job I've ever had properly. Whether it's the mail in ICI or working in an office pressing computers – and that's the scary thing. I must be a bit of a jobs-worth.'

Good Lord.

'It's the truth!' he hoots. 'I've fookin' made sure I've given it my all every time. I have to do things right and it's the same with singing. You're dying to laugh, aren't you? I know you are!'

Every weekend he'd take coach-trips to Manchester with his gang, hang around the station and the record shops. Went to gigs. Some mates formed a covers band, The Electric Crayon Set, with Tim singing, or rather screaming, Iggy Pop and Zeppelin tunes. Madchester was inventing itself. His mate Steve Harrison from the Omega Music record-shop told him about this new band, The Charlatans, and they went to see them. They had something, principally a groove-monster Hammond-organ nutter called Rob Collins, but they needed a proper frontman. Then the rubbish one left; Tim joined. In the summer of 1989 they wrote a song called 'The Only One I Know', put it out on their own Dead Dead Good label; it went straight to the top of the indie charts. The rest is hysteria/wilderness/hysteria and several billion sentences with the word 'lips' in them. And right now, those lips were made for drinking.

'I think we're getting a bit of a reputation for being drinkers, aren't we?' supposes Tim, ordering another bottle.

Well, yes you are, but then so's everybody else.

'It's getting serious,' notes Tim. 'Gets to me that, a bit – it's better to be a thinker than a drinker.'

Oh, you can be both.

'Well, yeah, you can be everything (massive grin). There's definitely something that's happened this year – everyone's just up for it! Don't know what it is. The brilliant tunes? Maybe you have to drink to do something brilliant. Which comes first?'

Tim loves his fags and booze. He once said, 'I love smoking, and I love drinking because it makes me smoke more.' He can open bottles of beer with his ear. The Charlatans have just returned from their latest American touring jamboree – 18 days and 10 gigs with Menswear. The two bands rapidly bonded and proceeded swiftly on to the rock 'n' roll diet of blow and bevvy – 'Menswear are brilliant, it was house-on-fire stuff. We all lost our minds a bit, heheh.'

Before they'd even landed The Charlatans were arrested – for enjoying themselves in the company of 'a tosser'. The bloke in front of Tim's seat objected to the beery tomfoolery behind, put his arms around the back of his seat, hands deliberately obliterating Tim's in-built TV screen.

'So me and Mark,' giggles Tim, 'started tickling his fingers.'

The bloke went berserk. Slammed Tim's seat, made a formal complaint to the appropriate authorities.

'So when we landed in New York,' says Tim, 'there was a Tannoy announcement saying the plane would be delayed while they waited for the police. They moved everyone out except us and the police came on and cuffed us all up. We got taken to the Port Authority cells. There'd been all these Chinese whispers that we were all swearing and spitting and smoking on a no-smoking flight, which was all lies. I was a bit scared, the guns and being cuffed and they're massive on planting stuff on you. They read us our rights, all this knobhead stuff. Got the FBI in. Took our passports off us and took our shoe-laces off us – don't know what that was for, I thought maybe it's just because they think we'll hang ourselves! (looks bemused) I wouldn't hang meself, I'm loving it at the moment, you can't put a downer on me!'

Three hours later the FBI pronounced the situation 'ridiculous' and freedom was granted.

Jail-bound or not, Tim loves the travelling, he loves America and he loves his new tattoo, taken from the *Daily Express* cartoon by Kelvin and Hobbs [*sic*]: 'I love it because it looks like he's asleep and he can't get out of bed. Tigers are top: they're ferocious and cuddly.' He also loves Chloe, his girlfriend of the last two years, the two years in which Tim's been happier that he's ever been before 'but never content: there's too much to be getting on with, but happiness is cool.' And so's being in love.

'Everything revolves around it,' notes Tim, 'everything that I do. Every day I consider Chloe's feelings. She inspires me. I think it's the best thing in the world. I really do.'

It's easy for him to fend off the inevitable lure of female fandom.

'I like meeting new people,' he states. 'I'm into it, but I'm also loyal and that makes people sick, but loyalty's cool. I think when you're loyal you have to question why (begins to crumble for no reason whatsoever). I think too much. Honest I do; I think too much all the time and I don't even know what I'm thinking about. I always thought that Timothy Burgess was a cool classical name but Martin Blunt was very sporty.'

Help.

'Chloe's me stabilizer,' says Tim, returning to the plot. 'She's mental but she's me voice of reason, she's a Taurus, a bit of a backbone. I've got a fully formed backbone, but there's someone there just needs to pull it from the back, an outer-puller. Oh God.'

Well, indeed.

'I'm so shit with words, me, I'm tellin' yer. No one fookin' ever understands a thing I say – now why is that?'

You're a somewhat bizarre conversationalist.

'No one gets what I mean or say,' says Tim, looking perplexed. 'They feel it but they don't get it. I wish I could be really . . . what's the word . . . integral and talk about proper stuff. I always imagine Jarvis Cocker to be really clever. I'm averagely statistical.'

He begins shouting, becomes finger-snappy demented.

'May Jarvis never die!' he shouts. 'He's one in a million! And I'm one in 10 (gales of laughter). Nah, I'm one in a million as well. I think. I don't know what I am, but I'm finding out.'

I doubt there's many of you in a pound.

'Honestly, just tell me,' he intones, 'just tell me what I am! Because I've not got a clue! I still don't know what the fuck's going on in my head.'

Have you always danced at all times, while sitting and walking, the lot?

'Yeah. It used to be with a hunch, but now I'm a bit straighter. Now why is that?'

Haven't got a clue, mate.

'I think people slouch when all they've got in the world is hatred. You straighten up when you've got something to celebrate.'

And he's got much to celebrate, not least being so good-looking it's preposterous. He's got those sweepy eyelashes that form semi-circles on the cheeks. His eyes are gigantic and ink black. The thick, dark hair. The snub nose. The famed lips. The perfect teeth. Must have a profound effect on your life, being beautiful. What does it feel like?

'Feels like nuthin',' he cringes, genuinely mortified. 'Dani Behr is officially classed as good-looking, but you wouldn't want to go out with her, would you? You'd hate her!'

There must be security in good looks: after all, people have killed themselves because they're ugly.

'Yeah, but I'm really . . . like in some relationships I'm really not self-assured at all. Seriously. I'm not into people for looks; I'm into what people get up to, what they kick up about, people who make a fuss. Rather than just sitting there being gorgeous. I don't even think I'm good-looking (begins flattening hair down into a deeply nerdy bowl-cut). I've never ever, ever fancied meself. Oh God, so what do I do? Is that weird? Do you think that's weird?'

I think everything's weird.

'I like records. I like records more than I like people! Hyickick!'

I go to the bathroom and leave Tim with the tape-recorder on in case he feels like telling a story. He does. And it goes like this:

'Hello. This is Tim. I'm going to tell a little wee story about the time we went to Sweden. It was top, right – we were playing on a little boat in Sweden sailing down the river and we got to the end of it and it was unbelievable right. Our sound geezer he got taken off the boat and he got slammed into prison and no one knows what the story is because it was kept really quiet and he's only just got out. The only problem with telling this story is that everyone in The Charlatans seems to have been in prison and that really worries me. Because I really want to be taken seriously for our music and I get scared sometimes that people don't take us seriously. And it's probably one of the hardest things in the whole world to get. But I think we're getting there. And all the devils inside me are beginning to turn into angels.'

Tim is a 'big-time insomniac' who often wakes up at 3 a.m. with the urge to wash all his clothes and have them ready for 6 a.m., whereupon he will hang them over the doors. He gets lost everywhere he goes; never been able to find his way back to the same place twice, 'not ever'. He reckons it's because he can't drive and he's used to being dropped off all the time. I reckon it's because taking responsibility for yourself is boring and there are more important things to think about.

'You're right,' he nods, 'but I'm too scared to admit it.'

He has two astonishingly distinct handwriting styles and whisks his Filofax out to prove it: one a beautifully neat, boxy, level set of capitals, the other a swirling extravagance – the work of two completely different souls.

Which one is the real you?

(Becoming incapable of speech) 'The real me ish the capicals.'

Tim was told by a woman he spoke to in San Francisco he was 'ultra-Gemini. She told me I was Geminied out me mind.' It seems we have the evidence. And now an alarm's gone off in his head. There's something he's not said and he must say it immediately. He switches the tape recorder back on.

'The Charlatans,' announces Tim, 'are at the forefront rather than the backfront of anything musical in the last fookin' 20 years. Everyone always thought of us as part of this Baggy scene and I always thought it was something different; you can drop out, do drugs and take over the world, that's what I thought it was, but everyone else thought it was baggy trousers. We're doing something that'll last for ever. I just want to be great, that's all. And now I've lost me credit card!'

You're an absolute nutter, Tim Burgess, you really are.

'I'm shorry! I really am shorry!'

Within three hours Tim will find himself comatose on his living room carpet. For my part, I will awake with a dodgy eye from a close-range arm-shooting incident, a limp to match his own and a lovely new watch for deep-sea diving with, several sizes too big. You don't just have a drink with Tim Burgess: you have a surreal and life-threatening experience. Meanwhile, he's too late for wishing he'll be great one day because he already is. And the new-born angels inside him know it.

Dr Joshi was cool and happy to help: 'Well, Tim, we shall just have to get you better.' For me and my compulsive personality, a 21-day detox – a strict diet with thirty herbal supplements a day – was perfect. I needed the order and the ritual. I took them at exactly the same time every day. It seemed like the obvious way to get a drug addict onto an alternative habit. After a few days the pills started to kick in and the thought of getting better started to sink in as well.

And then I went on tour, which was ideal because people were genuinely watching out for me. I didn't want the drink taken off the rider, I thought that would be too draconian to suggest to the band and would make me seem a little AA 12-step, but I did request my own room backstage.

It affected my performance immediately for the better. It had got to a point where I knew the songs were good, but the performances were letting me down in the studio and in the rehearsals. I had begun to feel like it was all a struggle.

The albums *Up at the Lake* and *Simpatico* were let down by the performances – not just my performances, but as I am supposed to lead then I only have myself to blame. I had got sloppy. Everybody knew. No one was telling me, but deep down I knew too.

Tony Linkin, our press officer at the time, but more importantly to me a friend, tried telling me in the nicest way he could, but there is only so much you can do. He definitely worried about me, though.

And Curly obviously knew, too. He knew that I wouldn't be able to do a world tour in the shape I was in. I was going through my Fat Elvis phase and in rehearsals I just couldn't sing without having a drink. A big fat line of bugle and a couple of bottles of wine, and I would be ready for a rehearsal. Then I would do a rehearsal and it would be shit. But I would carry on drinking throughout the day till I passed out, usually upstairs lying on the floor in front of the television, very often at 7 or 8 o'clock at night. Then I would wake up at two in the morning with the bottle there in front of me and I would fill my glass and start all over again.

I noticed the effects of the detox programme straight away. The singing on the tour got better with every show. Within three weeks, friends, co-workers and family started to say, 'Oh my God, Tim, you look really good.' Within three months,

I had lost ten pounds and shed ten years in looks and the way I felt.

Actually, the choice was simple. It was either music, which I got into the whole bloody thing for, or dropping out at the bottom and probably ending up on the streets. I noticed just in time to save my skin.

10. DIET COKE AND BANANAS

It's terrible when the suits get involved in rock 'n' roll. They are a bit like minders. They can be very useful, depending on what they are used for, but, as with minders, instead of sorting out a scuffle they can sometimes create more problems. They come between people who once communicated as friends and end up talking via third parties.

Alan McGee became The Charlatans' manager shortly after we'd met at the South by Southwest Festival in Austin, Texas, in

February 2006. South by Southwest is a showcase for everything that is new and cool about music, though at the time I was feeling neither new nor cool. I got myself cleaned up, and as part of that felt that having a new manager, and someone as experienced as Alan, was a good reason to take this second chance (or was it third, fourth, fifth? I don't know, you decide), get my shit together and rise to the occasion.

We had recorded *Simpatico* at Hook End Studios near Reading and were finishing mixing and overdubs at the Townhouse in London. Turmoil was in the air – not just with me personally, or even in the band, but with the whole musical landscape in general. At the time we were signed to Sanctuary, a label that turned out to be a disaster for us. The Townhouse was owned by Sanctuary and was rumoured to be shutting down. The walls seemed to be closing in around us.

Our A&R man John Williams had left just as we were about to deliver the record. The departure of the person who signed you is never a welcome moment for a band, but his parting gift was the resurrection of the Creole imprint, an old reggae label that was dusted down just for us.

Between 1999 and 2006 I had had an increasing number of meetings with prospective managers and couldn't find the right one – it was an unhappy time for me. During the making of *Simpatico* I had been trying to get an American manager to fly over to the UK to meet the band, but through fate or bad luck he never made it to England, and Curly Jobson took over temporarily. Steve Harrison had resigned after a particularly insulting email from me, written in conjunction with Michelle one Sunday evening in LA. I blamed Steve for the money going missing through our accountant. All the band believed he was responsible, of course! He was our manager and the buck stopped there.

Back to McGee, as I want to keep this brief. He was the man who had made his name with Oasis, so he was no stranger to the nuttier side of life. After coming off drugs and touring *Simpatico* around the world, I went on a DJ tour with McGee in October 2006. We called it the Diet Coke and Banana tour. This was a manager/artist bonding trip, set up so that we could get to know each other properly and work out the next few years for the band.

There seemed to be a change in the air of how to go about things which really appealed to both of us. We were avid social networkers, and the whole tour had been arranged, promoted and documented on Myspace. The use of internet for self-promotion was gathering pace. With what seemed like only people power, The Arctic Monkeys had come out of nowhere to be the biggest new band in Britain. And Alan, fresh from managing The Libertines, was impressed with Pete Doherty, a self-promoting extremist and one of the few people Alan acknowledges as more controversial than him.

Having a masochistic bent, I loved the idea that Pete put his recordings up on the internet for all to see. These were more often than not scratch and live recordings, demos and half-written ideas, but they were used as a new, unorthodox promotional tool. The fans loved it. These were the early signs that record companies were not needed to get songs out to the world.

CD sales were at an all-time low and record shops were becoming like ghost towns. People were plundering the internet for music, using peer-to-peer file-sharing sites, and the figures of estimated sharing were getting higher by the month. (At the time of the release of *You Cross My Path*, our next LP, the peer-to-peer sharing estimate was 1:60, which means that, for every CD or download of a record bought legally, it was shared illegally for free by sixty others.) The times they were a-changing.

During the DJ tour we stumbled on the idea that the best way to get The Charlatans' new material to people at this watershed moment was to give it away. We were more comfortable with the idea of giving it away before it was inevitably taken. We considered all the options: re-signing to Sanctuary, going with another label, forming our own label, but throughout our jaunt around Britain we came to the conclusion that giving it away was the most exciting thing to do. It was far out for an established band, but anything less seemed like a cop-out. In some ways it seemed obvious, though it made me question our sanity slightly – it was hard to know what was the right thing to do, but to everyone's eternal credit *You Cross My Path* came out for free.

We made our own stipulations. It had to be the best album we could make; we had to give it away to as many people as possible; and we had to go into it wholeheartedly. At one point McGee suggested giving it away with the *Sun*, but the band had misgivings. Bizarrely, Prince had given away his album with the *Mail on Sunday*, which conjures up thoughts of thousands of untouched, abandoned CDs behind the twitching net curtains of middle England. I'm not sure who was advising him there.

Prince had given his away to pensioners. We gave ours away through Xfm: over 150,000 downloads from one site and an unknown number of file shares from there. Radiohead sold their album *In Rainbows* through a pay-what-you-like scheme requiring, shrewdly, the purchaser's email address for future data. We gave ours away with a radio station and asked for zero info. Dumb? A missed trick? We didn't care.

McGee and I were on *News at Ten*. It was a phenomenon. This was the first time we had been judged on an action and not on the material. But the record was great.

Juliette Garside, *Sunday Telegraph*, October 2007:

> Supporting a rock band used to be an act of rebellion. In the face of today's mounting music piracy, it's become an act of conscience.
>
> Radiohead, the contrarian giants of British rock, last week

released their seventh album on an unsuspecting public with the challenge of paying as little or as much as they choose. *In Rainbows* is available on the internet only, and the only compulsory charge is a 45p credit card handling fee.

In the same week indie legends The Charlatans went one better and made their new single 'You Cross My Path' available from radio station Xfm's website at no charge.

'I want the people to own the music and the artists to own the copyright. Why let a record company get in the way of the music?' says Tim Burgess, The Charlatans' lead singer.

These gestures are without doubt a two-fingered salute to the fat cats at the major record labels. More worryingly for the four international companies that account for 80 per cent of worldwide music sales they could also sound the death knell for paid-for music.

[. . .]

When Prince wanted to publicize his 21-night residency at London's O2 arena, he distributed his album as a covermount on a national newspaper. Artists with international pulling power are using the physical CD as a sampler for the new money-spinner – box office sales.

[. . .]

Alan McGee, who made Oasis a household name when he ran Creation Records and now manages The Charlatans says: 'It is definitely the beginning of the end of the old model.'

Ian Burrell, *Independent*, October 2007:

Alan McGee, the musical impresario behind Oasis, has hatched an audacious plan to make new singles and albums available to download free, a move that threatens to throw the music industry into confusion.

Speaking from Los Angeles, McGee said he decided to give The Charlatans' music away for free after they were offered a deal he considered less than satisfactory by their record company,

Sanctuary. 'I thought: "Well nobody buys CDs anyway". If you talk to a 19-year-old kid, they don't buy CDs [. . .] I came to the conclusion: "Why don't we just give it away for nothing?" '

[. . .]

The radical approach of The Charlatans follows the decision by Prince to distribute an estimated 3 million copies of his latest album with *The Mail on Sunday*, driving ticket sales for his record breaking series of concerts at London's O2 arena. The Charlatans have opted for a more ground-breaking approach, to put it on a radio station website, where it can be downloaded for free at anytime.

McGee said the band 'could not lose' from the revolutionary approach.

[. . .]

Mike Walsh, the head of music at Xfm, said the download service, which starts on 22 October, would remain active 'for as long as there's demand'. He said: 'We thought it was an irresistible opportunity to do something that had not been done before.'

★ ★ ★

Alan McGee found himself managing Carl Barât's new band, Dirty Pretty Things. He had very briefly managed The Libertines before their final cataclysmic implosion and was left with the bits of the jigsaw that made up Albion's favourite sons.

So let's talk about Carl. He was most celebrated as Pete's oppo in The Libertines and had been drawn into the tabloid whirlwind that surrounded his other half – thrown up in the air and dropped back down again when the tabloids had had their use of him.

I met Carl in the bar of the Trafalgar Hotel, in London. I'd ended up back there after The Charlatans had just played Heaven, the infamous gay club behind Charing Cross Station. There is nothing quite like playing a stage on which you've previously witnessed an amazing gig. I'd seen New Order there in 1984.

The Libertines had recently completed the video for 'Don't Look Back into the Sun'. This was not the first time I had come across the band – I had seen them play live in a club in Brick Lane and hadn't really liked them very much, but I might have been drunk and a touch angry.

Carl was a Gemini. I was a Gemini. I felt we bonded. We were friendly from the off, sussing each other out. We were both looking for something exciting to do that night but nothing really happened, and I went to bed while Carl wandered the streets of London.

I sensed that Carl was as lost as me, and it brought us together. I had come to the conclusion that I was lost living in LA. In a moment all the things that were good about it became all the things that were bad about it: the brightness and politeness, everyone hidden behind sunglasses. It had taken me a while to realize that the smiles were provided by Vicodin, OxyContin and Xanax. When I did, it gave me a greater understanding of David Lynch films, but unfortunately I felt that I was living in one.

I was happy in a Stepford Wives kind of way. I had a house in Hollywood overlooking the sign, an idyllic set-up at the time. I had a wife, a dog and lots of friends. Deep down, though, I was uncertain about everything. That was the only thing I *was* certain of.

I was in a permanent state of jet-lag haze. I never seemed to be at home, and everything important felt so far away. The band all seemed to be enjoying their lives with their families, having kids; perhaps we were moving apart as our circumstances became so different. We were still writing together, but there seemed to be no gang mentality. Every time we gathered, something in the band spirit seemed to get watered down. Business was always the last thing on our minds, and anyway my main business now was drugs.

I was becoming ever more agitated, bloated and bleary-eyed.

Meanwhile our manager was broke, so we suspected he wasn't in the best place to make decisions for us as we were his only income.

The band and the manager, their world and their lifestyle, seemed completely alien to me, and I began to feel, as Johnny Thunders rightfully put it, So Alone.

Carl was lost, too, because his band mate and co-writer was struggling with heroin. Doherty had burgled Carl's flat, served a stretch at Her Majesty's Pleasure, and was now trying to get clean in Thailand with help from Dot Cotton of *EastEnders*. You couldn't make it up.

We were helping each other. Carl felt he was losing his co-writer and I had lost mine eight or nine years ago and was still in mourning. We spent quality time together in Paris. I was staying at the Terrace Hotel in Montmartre. On Valentine's Day 2004 Carl and his girlfriend Annalisa came over for a drink. We went off for a stroll in the charming surroundings and I ended up rolling down a hill. We definitely brought out the best in each other — or is that the worst?

I took him to the Isle of Wight Festival and introduced him on stage, as The Libertines were supposed to have been playing that weekend. Carl thought it would be helpful for him to go. We had a great time, drinking vodka and orange, and surfing the bus — heads out of the skylight, hair blowing in the wind, in an exact point between *Titanic* and *Every Which Way but Loose*. Was he sitting with Pete? Was I sitting with Rob?

We laughed about how I had a band mate from West Bromwich. He had a band member who loved Albion.

One day Carl popped unannounced into my room in the Premier Inn in King's Cross. I loved that about him. Everyone else I knew made arrangements, days in advance, but Carl had no calendar. He was old school — a young man with older ways.

I took him for pizza, we drank red wine and had a wrestling match in my room — not naked or in front of the fire, but there was a touch of the Oliver Reed and Alan Bates about us.

I began to notice that I was getting drunker so much more

easily and quickly, and had no recollection of events the morning after. I was waking up in unpromising situations, on the floor mostly, though occasionally my drunken SatNav would direct me to the nearest bed, with no concern for whose it was. I definitely had no intentions but to pass out. Somewhere in the back of my mind I'd think I was at home, somewhere else in the back of my mind I knew I was in trouble.

On this occasion I woke up at the Premier Inn with a huge red wine stain on the carpet. This was not subtle. Ashtrays were on the floor, there were cigarette butts everywhere, the TV was on, the curtains were open, clothes everywhere. This was my life now, this was the way I had chosen to live.

I'd agreed to meet photographer Tom Sheehan and journalist Dominic Wills that afternoon for lunch and drinks. Both of them had documented the band since 1990. By all accounts I was incoherent after two pints, topping up from the night before. I hadn't seen Dominic for a few years, maybe five, and he apparently told Tom I was unrecognizable to him as the person he knew. Like I said, I was just topping up.

I went back to LA and Michelle. Her yin was my yang. I was exhausted, yes partly from drinking, but also from all the work I was doing: gigs, DJing, radio, TV, general promo work.

Don't get me wrong – I am not whingeing here. But my life was just two speeds: stop and full on. I would go home hoping to rest and get rid of my hangover. Michelle was excited to see me and wanted to go out and show the world she had a husband. She must have felt like an army wife at times.

I knew I would never succumb to what are known as groupies. But I suppose she could never be sure. She had said to me that if it was unavoidable, I was just not to fall in love. But, if the truth be told, it never crossed my mind. Sorry if you bought this book thinking it would be loaded with sex. Instead I filled my time with drugs and rock 'n' roll.

★ ★ ★

I had been asked to do a solo gig in Chatham at the Tap and Tin pub, made famous as the scene of The Libertines' reunion gig, by a friend, the very charming Dean Fragile. Carl promised to play guitar for me, and he was a man of his word. Alongside us for the night Carl recruited Martin Duffy from Primal Scream and Andy Burrows from Razorlight. We called ourselves The Chavs.

At the time The Charlatans were rehearsing with Ronnie Wood for a *Dazed and Confused* party called Hero to Hero – the magazine had approached us and him and, naturally, we jumped at the chance. The event was going to take place at the Shepherd's Bush Empire the following night and the opening act would be Babyshambles, Pete Doherty's side-project turned main band because of the circumstances with Carl. Kate Moss would be there. The Chavs – the band that Carl and I were both moonlighting in – were rehearsing upstairs in the kitchen with a bass drum and a broken Wurlitzer keyboard. We were supposed to be picked up there in 'Rocks off' Ross's cadillac, organized by Mr Fragile. We didn't ask for it, we didn't want it, and anyway we never got it. What we did get was a red Toyota Corolla with no back window and bits of glass on the seat. That's better, right?

I was impressed by Andy Burrows: he knew the Charlatans and Libertines songs we were about to perform, better than me and Carl in fact. We were so caught up in the excitement that I don't think we knew our songs at all. Duffy was just laughing constantly, wondering what the hell was going on and thinking of as many alternative names for The Chavs as possible – The Chillblains being the most applauded and the funniest sounding in a Brummie accent. But The Chavs it was, since we were playing Chatham and 'chav' was the word of the moment.

Opening that night, the Buff Medways featured former

Milkshake, Mighty Caesar and chief Headcoat Wild Billy Childish, with Graham Day from The Prisoners and Wolf Howard from The Daggermen. Billy gave me a signed book and we had our picture taken together for the *Medway Standard*.

Michelle was our cheerleader and wrote out our set-list:

I Believe in the Spirit
Road to Ruin
North Country Boy
I Get Along
Death on the Stairs
A Man Needs to Be Told
France
Fairytale of New York

As you can imagine, the under-rehearsed gig was shambolic, but it was beautiful too. Tony Linkin, who was the publicist for Carl, Pete and The Charlatans, told me that his face ached from laughing so much. I'm not sure that's the feedback anyone in a band appreciates, but for one night only we were free to be whatever we wanted, and it felt good.

★ ★ ★

Alan McGee moved to Hollywood, to a hotel on Sunset Boulevard, and started hanging around with Lisa Marie Presley, although he claimed he didn't know who she was at first. He said the same thing about Joaquin Phoenix, though I'm not sure who else he thought they were. They seemed to be treated like Hollywood royalty by everyone else. At the same time he was trying desperately to avoid becoming the manager of Courtney Love, though he did become, briefly, the manager for ultra-cool outfit Spinnerette.

Tony Kaye, who had directed *American History X*, sensed

some controversy and wanted to make a film about what we were doing.

★ ★ ★

So we made the album *You Cross My Path*. Did I tell you it was very good?

We thought the simplest idea for the cover would be a black cat. Superstitious folk in some countries say that a black cat is lucky, but in others it's deemed unlucky. We thought we couldn't lose, as we had seen our fair share of both and were prepared for whatever was still to be thrown at us.

I asked Faris Badwan, from my favourite upcoming band The Horrors, to design it. I felt that at the tender age of 21 he was fast becoming one of Britain's most interesting artists. He had a small exhibition on in Brick Lane, and his drawing of a raven caught my attention, maybe because the raven to me represents Rob Collins – his neighbour used to call him Raven, perhaps because of his long black hair and his shadowy lurching frame (Rob, that is, not Faris).

Faris did a couple of drawings, one of a single cat and one of five, representing each member of the band. I still have fun trying to figure out who is who – but I think I know. Shall we have a look at the songs?

1. 'Oh Vanity'

This modern look at our old influences, part New Order part Booker T, was written on Logic, the band-friendly alternative to Pro Tools. Tony Rogers was becoming an extremely proficient user of this computer software, so I got the program and taught myself between tours how to use it.

I wrote 'Oh Vanity' in preparation for Tony and Mark coming out to Los Angeles. They came for a couple of weeks, renting an apartment which we used as a base. We were about to begin writing for our post-modern, post-punk giveaway album. Alan McGee was there to oversee manoeuvres and feed the troops. It seemed appropriate to write in an apartment building on the corner of Sunset and Vine, because 'Sunset and Vine' had been the final instrumental track on our previous album. It felt like a seamless move from the past to the present.

Tony took the song up a level by programming a Sly Stone/PIL/Stone Roses-style drum beat and an Irish jig-style Hammond organ solo. It has a singalong chorus with no words. Mark added bass line and guitar chugs, and Jon and Martin overdubbed their bits at the Big Mushroom studios that The Charlatans call home.

Douglas Hart directed the video, which features Peaches Geldof. Douglas's script read, 'Like the end of *Carrie*. Without all the blood.'

2. 'Bad Days'

Tony and Martin supplied the intro melody, the words 'I get these bad days, baby', and the opening main bass line. I supplied the high-note Hooky-style bass guitar solo, the 'playing dead under the covers' and 'Oh! we could never be desperate' bits. In the *Independent*, Andy Gill described the track as 'skittish disco hi-hats, striding bass and electropop synth motif . . . a dig at a former friend'.

Who am I to argue?

I love using the high falsetto vocal on songs with such negative-feeling lyrics. It makes the balance of sweet with sour, a pinch of sugar to balance the lime juice. The 'playing dead under the covers' bits remind me of The Cure.

3. 'Mis-takes'

This was a Northern song. Although I was living in LA I was still singing Northern songs. 'Mis-takes' is about breaking up with someone. I suppose I was predicting my imminent obvious-to-everyone-around-me split with Michelle, though this wasn't to happen for a few years yet. Songs often reveal their true meaning to the writer long after they were written.

Owing to band commitments, Michelle and I had found ourselves living at the K West Hotel in Shepherd's Bush for about six months. Hotels encapsulate lots of the elements of what people see as a rock 'n' roll lifestyle, and they can be the catalyst for madness and excess. They are something that in a more regular life would be confined to short stays, with relaxation as their primary purpose. But extend a stay and throw in the pressure of making an album or the lunacy of being on a tour, and they are hothouses for weirdness.

When people in music mention hotels, images of trashed rooms and TVs chucked out of the window spring to mind. But in this case it was as close to Alan Partridge's lengthy sojourn at the Tipton Travel Tavern as it was to the members of Led Zep living it up at the Riot House.

The K West is a plain, dark, forbidding building, with a permanent smell of sauna and a reception like a train station during rush hour, but my mood wasn't governed by the hotel, more by my general state of mind. The only way to get to your room was to walk right through the main bar – the hotel attracted lots of music-business types and bands, so the chances were that any time you went from the reception to your room or from your room to outside, someone would call out your name. They'd announce how we'd not spent time together in ages and how right now was the time to remedy that situation with a couple of drinks. One of the residents was William Reid, who was staying there for two weeks while The Jesus and Mary Chain rehearsed for their comeback shows.

When I was out making the record he, Michelle and Evan Dando's manager would pass the time together, ordering bottles of vodka and champagne, entertaining whoever was in town.

I was beginning to feel like a stranger in my own hotel room.

I left Michelle a few times during this period, though I am not sure if it ever registered. One time I left her and went up to Birmingham, recorded a song with Tony, came back down to the hotel – and she was still partying, completely unaware that I had even gone. This was not fun! It was dark.

McGee remembers at least two occasions when I went over to his house just to get away from the madness. When you're heading to Alan McGee's for peace and quiet then you know something needs looking at.

'Mis-takes' is sourced from a cross between 'Regret' and 'Sooner Than You Think' by New Order, and 'Catch' by The Cure. Tony's beautiful backing vocals make this song for me. Jon recorded his drums in Tony's front room.

4. 'The Misbegotten'

This was inspired by the work of Diane Arbus, one of my favourite photographers and writers, noted for her black and white square photographs of deviant and marginal people, dwarfs, giants, transvestites, nudists and circus performers, or of people whose normality seems ugly or surreal. The sleeve of the single was a direct reconstruction of 'Two Girls in Matching Bathing Suits', using friends as models. I hope I did a better job than Martin did with the *Up to Our Hips* front cover.

It was inspired musically by Doris Norton, an electronic computer pioneer, whose album *Personal Computer* is some kind of missing link between Kraftwerk and New Order. It's a beautiful record – I have a signed copy.

Lyrically, I used the cut-up technique of William Burroughs, later picked up by David Bowie.

There are stories to be told and stories that are just too creepy for comfort. This one is on the cusp, but here goes. I was at a party in a hotel one night and a guy from Aberdeen came up to me and told me that his wife was a big fan and he would never let anyone else touch her, but if I wanted to, he said I could 'have sex with her'. He was trying to be friendly and offer me something he would never offer anyone else, but I was a little freaked out! I wonder what she would have said about it? Maybe she knew, maybe she didn't, maybe it was her idea and they were a couple of swingers. It wouldn't be the first time I had been proposed to like that. He said he was a poet.

I changed 'fuck his wife' to 'change his life' in the final cut-up version of the song.

5. 'A Day for Letting Go'

This song was written at home in LA, mostly influenced by girl group The Shangri-Las, but musically it doesn't really matter. It's all about the changes in the melody and the lyrics. Here are the lyrics:

> It's a day for letting go,
> You've lost all the control,
> Burn a bridge, call me a bitch,
> Start tearing up each other's clothes.

To the only world who'd know,
It's a day for letting go,
Elevate me, eventually now,
Heads are gonna roll.

I want you to be happy,
So fair and brotherly
And evidently,
Everything depends upon the drug.

I bit into a wall,
You could have given more,
With repetition,
It begs the question which side are you on?

The feeling never goes,
You suffocate my soul,
Revenge is sweet, and
Bitterness will seep into our little bones.

I want you to be happy,
So fair and brotherly
And evidently,
Everything depends upon the drug.

You wouldn't want to be with me alone,
With the subs,
When you reach out, in your sleep as a youth,
Oh, you wouldn't wanna get me on the rock,
This is the sound, of the crowd, and our dreams
   burning down.

Inoculate my soul,
Whose side are you on?
Evidently everything depends upon the drug.

6. 'You Cross My Path'

Alan McGee said to me that this was the most brutal track he'd heard since 'Upside Down' by The Jesus and Mary Chain. While listening to 'Circus of Death' by Human League it occurred to me that it sounded exactly the same as 'Sunrise' by New Order.

It was the perfect template for unleashing all my pent-up anger about anyone who got in my way.

I was angry. I only snap once in a while; with this song I snapped. I still sing like a nasally kid, though. I used biblical references and lines from *The Exorcist*. I wanted it to be our 'Sympathy for the Devil', but of course it sounds nothing like it. I was interested in creating a similar vibe, not re-creating the Stones' song.

Me and McGee were always imagining doing the free album with Youth, bass player for Killing Joke and producer of choice for Paul McCartney, Crowded House and Siouxsie and The Banshees. But when McGee finally heard the demo of this track, he screamed to me 'Alan Moulder!' He was referring to the producer/mixer who'd shaped albums by The Yeah Yeah Yeahs and Curve and had played a massive part in the recording of *Loveless*.

I was ecstatic. I had wanted to work with him all my musical life, yet for some reason I thought he wasn't keen on us. Once McGee had mooted the idea, I couldn't imagine anyone else for the job. I couldn't get another producer into my head. So McGee was duly dispatched to rope him in. I had that weird sensation in my stomach when excitement kicks in and rationality all but goes out of the window.

Moulder rang me up at home in LA and told me how he would like to approach mixing the track. He loved it! What you hear is Alan Moulder's mix of our demo.

The video was made by my friend Charles Mehling, one of the very first people I met in LA when I moved there. He was the bass guitarist for underground LA legends Brian Jonestown Massacre. When he left the band he took up being the lighting engineer for Black Rebel Motorcycle Club – BRMC supported us on our US tour in 2001. Charles began to make their videos and he found his calling.

He is now one of the most sought-after music-video directors around, but he did 'You Cross My Path' for a mate's-rate fee, a tenth of what he normally charged.

7. *'Missing Beats (of a Generation)'*

This is pretty much Tony Rogers's song; I just added the words. It's about youthful sex, the way things turn out, expectations and disappointment. Wow! I gave it everything. And I was happy that I'd managed to get DNA into the lyrics, as well as a melody reference to my first ever single by The Cure, 'Primary'.

8. *'My Name is Despair'*

Opening with a sample of Crass's 'Reality Asylum' mixed in with street noise from Manchester, this was originally a jam by Martin and Jon. I rewrote it back in LA.

While writing this I had the idea of *The Gothic Wild West* as the title for the album, but it wasn't a goer as far as the band were concerned. I wanted to reference the southern American Gothic tradition of writing, from William Faulkner to Thomas Wolfe and the art of Grant Wood, all of it soundtracked by Gram Parsons. Gram was almost the personification of Gothic tragedy. His family was wealthy, but his family tree was rife with suicide, insanity and alcoholism. His own life unfolded like a tragic Tennessee Williams play.

I thought it was an interesting idea, but other people just thought – The Horrors. Maybe I was barking up the wrong tree, but I thought this track sounded like Gothic country post-punk, or Johnny Cash's American albums.

Anyway, with my Indian war cry, hand on mouth, and Alan Moulder's genius mix I think we created the album's centrepiece and perhaps the band's darkest work to date.

9. *'Bird Reprise'*

This is my personal favourite from the record because it is so intentionally small after the mammoth 'My Name is Despair'.

There was a part of my soul that was dying at this point in my life.

I was trying to write the final song for the album in Los Angeles, and I didn't leave my room for a whole week. It took me that long to write the shortest song I've sung.

I feel really happy with it. Emotionally, the music and lyrics are in harmony with each other, something I had been really striving for. The feeling is best summed up by that word '*simpatico*', a term I had seen Keith Richards use in a book when describing The Rolling Stones' relationship with their producer Jimmy Miller.

'Bird' is in my Top 5 Charlatans songs of all time.

> I wish I could die in your arms tonight.
> There is a part of me leaving
> Believing the hype.
> I wish I was a bird
> Wouldn't that be absurd

To flap at your window
To breathe you the word.

10. *'This is the End'*

I was thinking about The Chameleons' song 'Tears'. If you don't own a copy of *Strange Times* by The Chameleons, get one now – it's one of my favourite albums from 1986. There are also bits of Wordsworth and Paul Anka in the lyrics, and we wanted to capture the mood of 'The End' by The Doors. Tony Rogers sang beautiful backing vocals, as good as Rob Collins had done.

I wanted to write a song that signposted something more than just the last song on the album. Each listener will think of his own endings, but for me this was a time of endings.

I think it was the end of LA for me, to be honest.

* * *

Some albums get defined by the landscape around them as much as how they sound. We had often been included in movements like Baggy and Britpop without setting out to sound like what was going on around us. Albums are written, recorded and released over a period of time of anything up to three years and it is sometimes merely by chance that a 'scene' evolves. The musical landscape before the release of *You Cross My Path* was changing, much of it for the better.

In the pre-punk era, instruments were prohibitively expensive and studios were the size of small towns, with the result that public-school oldboys like Genesis ended up soundtracking the times. By 2006, Myspace, Garageband and the rest had changed the landscape – choices were taken away from labels and handed direct to kids. Being able to advertise gigs without relying on traditional adverts, posters and fliers meant that young promoters could make a play for taking over.

It seemed that younger kids were becoming fans of music that had previously been aimed at the over-18s. A wage wasn't needed to have a record collection. Not even records were needed. The Underage Festival and the under-18s gigs up and down the country represented a massive shift in who was making music and who it was being made for. Bands and festivals seemed to be flourishing.

★ ★ ★

Joaquin Phoenix told the *NME,* 'Holy fucking shit, the Charlatans record is mega. A real beauty. I can't wait to see it live.'

Alan introduced Glasvegas to Lisa Marie and off they went towards Elvis.

Me, Mcgee, Joaquin and Antony Langdon made a record together.

Back in the UK after not very much at all, really, except a worldwide tour in support of our best LP since 2004, Alan quit the music industry, and just like that our relationship was over. The day after, he sent in his team of pit bulls to sort everything out.

When things go sour with people it's sometimes hard to know the source of the problems, and what happened with Alan McGee is testament to this. Everything seemed OK, then all hell broke loose. I'd say it was handled maturely, but some of it revolved around an 'unfriending' on Myspace, so it's undeniable that part of it was petty. Spats in the world of music are often ugly and they can break out in public. Like a playground scrap, but at a stage school, and there's usually at least one person drunk.

Alan quit managing the band without notice just before a

European tour. It was when we reached Berlin that the shit hit the fan. I figured he'd just fallen out with me, and he said as much in a phone call.

Now a book like this can be an opportunity for revelation, and the band's lawyer and accountant will no doubt be hoping I reveal exactly what went on between me and Alan, or me, Michelle and Alan, but I have to admit I have almost no idea. McGee emailed me while I was in Europe without internet access for a couple of days. When I finally got his message, it said something like, 'Get in touch or there is going to be trouble.' I told him that I couldn't get in touch as I was on a tour bus in Europe with very limited internet access, and that I didn't regard this as a message you got from a friend.

Michelle and McGee were both big on social networking, especially Myspace. Michelle would sometimes go on it when she shouldn't, especially when she'd had a drink, and stir things up. They would wind each other up and be competitive in a jokey way, but it seemed to get out of hand and they had some kind of disagreement. I thought it had been coming for ages – both were volatile and competitive, and neither would step back. Michelle accused me of not sticking up for her, of believing McGee over her, and blaming her for things she hadn't done. We didn't speak for a week. There's nothing worse than being on tour and falling out with your girl.

As with any falling out, it's hard to say what really happened. McGee claimed that Michelle had been saying negative things about his family. I don't know. Perhaps Michelle and Alan know. But I will never get the chance to ask them now, so it will always remain a mystery.

McGee went from being passive to aggressive at the click of an alt-cmd-delete instruction. Our friendship was over and everything between us unravelled. Before long he had a club night with Noel and Liam's brother Paul Gallagher, then he announced his retirement from music altogether. The air has never been fully cleared and the only thing for sure is that McGee was a major part in The Charlatans' story, and I hope we have a place in his.

★ ★ ★

When people in music are in their hedonistic prime there is little time for anything else, as the fun of drink and drugs is all-consuming. You're having a brilliant time but you have little regard for anyone more than shouting distance away.

The most obvious way of curtailing the rock star lifestyle is by checking out of the hotel completely, through a premature death that ironically can confer some kind of immortality. The very thing that was providing someone with all their enjoyment is what finishes them off.

Every so often a titan of excess does come along who, having spent a lifetime of living it up, restores our faith in the debauchery of rock stars. For most of us, though, a change has to come, and if it does, you're sure to hear about it via the medium of a book!

Everyone needs a saviour. The old me would have looked at something like transcendental meditation and dismissed it as a kookie pastime taken up by people who had lost their edge. The fact that the David Lynch Foundation was involved, though, sparked my interest.

Music history is full of people living life to the full and then either dying, going mad or discovering something else completely. I remember reading about Roger McGuinn of The Byrds becoming a born-again Christian and reverting to his original name of Jim. I thought it'd be cool to live a life of excess and then give it all up to be a born-again Christian or even join a cult. But when the time came for me, the dogma and baggage of religion didn't appeal, and most of the cults I'd come across had too many weird rules.

I had done the giving up, which left a gap, not necessarily a spiritual or emotional gap, but certainly a practical one. Sourcing and ingesting drink and drugs takes longer than you think; now I was rising earlier in the morning, which freed up a surprising amount of time.

It wasn't religion or even transcendental meditation that I was particularly looking for. I would have been just as happy if that thing had turned out to be steam engines and a Casey Jones hat – as it had been for Pete Waterman.

These things have a strange way of finding you. I suppose I had a demeanour and body language that suggested I was on the lookout for something. I had thrown a party at my flat on Hoxton Square in East London and, as ever, was happy to be around friends who were still drinking and living it up – to be fair, they had probably never taken to that side of things with the professional vigour that I had, so there was little need for them to exorcize alcohol and drugs from their lives.

I was happy to watch everyone enjoying themselves and took a seat that gave me a good view. My friend Amy came to sit beside me and we exchanged the regular pleasantries. She was enjoying a glass of wine, looked as cool as everyone else and most people at the party knew her. She didn't seem different from them and certainly didn't come across as someone who had practised TM since she was 4 years old. Now, I'm not exactly sure what someone who had studied TM since they were 4 would look like, but the character that Britt Ekland played in *The Wicker Man*, and the song she sang, would probably have captured it. Anyway, Amy seemed to notice my detachment and asked if I'd ever considered TM.

Often at parties conversations just go in one ear and out of the other – someone has discovered the new Beatles, a new drug is doing the rounds, someone has said something sharp about someone else. But this went in one ear and stuck around. I'd been made redundant from my regular employment at a party, so I had time to listen. I was intrigued, and Amy continued. She had grown up in Skelmersdale, the unlikely home of the TM movement in the UK, and she thought that it was something that could benefit me.

The old me would have been knee-deep in the goings-on at the party, but Amy had a poise and aura which held my attention. She was enjoying the evening but wasn't consumed by it. The very next day I found myself talking to her guru, Will, who was based on the Isle of Wight. It was exactly what I was looking for, and I've now been meditating twice a day for three years.

I'm not on commission for getting new recruits. One of the things it's made me realize is that everyone needs something but what that something is differs from person to person. This was mine.

Recently I did an interview about TM and afterwards the interviewer sent me an email. I was hoping that I'd explained it in such a way that he had been inspired to ask more about the inner peace it brings and the way he could use it in his life. It was no such thing. His digital recorder had not been working. The message read, 'Soz about Dictaphone breaking, mate. What was that transatlantic levitation you were saying about?' Make what you will of that.

The transcendental meditation technique is a totally pure tradition governed by nature. I don't have to do very much, I just do the meditation and let life take care of itself. It feels right for me. The important thing is to make it a habit, to integrate it into daily life. And if there's one thing I've proved it's that I can develop a habit and keep it up.

Clint Eastwood, The Beatles, Lou Reed, Donovan, Russell Brand and David Lynch are all exponents, so I figured it wasn't going to turn me into a loopy Hollywood nut job. David Lynch was possibly the biggest influence on me taking up TM. Whatever made this man tick, I wanted some. He'd been my favourite film-maker from the first time I saw *Blue Velvet*, tracing back to *Eraserhead* and the freakily unfathomable *Mulholland Drive*. It was perhaps his use of music in film that attracted me – or the fact that his films were so enigmatic and contain some of the most shocking and outrageous sensual and sexual images on screen. My mind races through episodes of *Twin Peaks*, and the slow dreamlike pace indicates to me that it was a meditative piece. That was the appeal of the series for me.

When you mention TM, the first things that spring to most people's minds are the bearded Beatles, the Maharishi Mahesh Yogi and orange-toga'd bell-clangers walking down Oxford Street. It's generally lumped in with all kinds of other eastern mysticism. Rob Collins used to have a video called *The Compleat Beatles*. We used to watch it almost every time I stayed over at his house in Bloxwich. He would sit in his chair by the record player with his slippers on, smoking a Benson and Hedges, a reassuringly old man at the age of what? 24? We would put it on either when there was nothing else to watch or at the end of the night, when his wife had gone to bed – and we'd get caught up in the excitement of the cult potential.

So it was through Rob that I first became aware of the Maharishi. TM is a part of my everyday life and I'm as happy as I've ever been, still in touch with the old me but relieved too that my life has changed. I'm still the person that sat with Rob, but I feel less blown around by outside forces. I watch some performances now on DVD and I can remember little of them. What got me through was something I couldn't keep doing for ever. I suspect it stopped just in time.

* * *

I've always loved working with other bands since we first got together as The Charlatans, but the band itself has also enjoyed welcoming guests for short stays from time to time – sometimes for a couple of songs, like Johnny Marr at Wembley Arena on 'Right On' and 'Weirdo', sometimes for ten songs, as with Ronnie Wood at the Hero to Hero gig, and sometimes for an entire tour, as in the case of Pete Salisbury. Our alumni also include Denise Johnson from Primal Scream, who joined us for 'Power to the People' at a Manchester Versus Cancer show, where we also did 'A Town Called Malice' with Paul Weller. Everyone from Dirty Pretty Things helped out on an Adam and The Ants cover we did for a TV show.

I've hardly mentioned Paul Weller in this book up to now, but The Modfather has had a role in my story pretty much permanently since 1979 – he soundtracks a lot of it and later pops up as a friend who I played songs alongside, a figure I looked up to, a songwriter as important as John Lennon, and an angry young man who came spitting out of my parents' radio in Moulton. It's something that gets forgotten, but TV and radio now are so audience-driven that it's unlikely that different generations will listen to the same radio programme or watch TV pop shows together. Houses with multiple TVs were a rarity back then, so teens up and down the land would aim to earn enough brownie points from their parents to get their choice of programme at 7.20 on a Thursday evening.

And so it was in 1979 that Weller, along with Buckler and Foxton, gatecrashed our suburban living room. Fast forward the tape nearly thirty years and I am with Weller in his dressing room after his Hollywood gig. Catherine Zeta Jones and Steve Coogan are there, and there is something of a Brits-done-good feel to the party.

I'd always been a fan of his music and he seemed quite surprised when I told him. I'd liked every stage of Weller's career. It's funny, but it seems natural to call him by his surname when writing about him. 'Paul' just doesn't sound big enough; a bit like calling Bowie, 'David'.

I took a copy of The Jam's 'Funeral Pyre' and The Style Council's *Á Paris* EP for him to sign – I've never shied away from getting records signed. I've got them all – The Rolling Stones, The Who, The Clash, Mark E. Smith, Throbbing Gristle, The Libertines, The Horrors, New Order . . .

It's weird, I'd have thought he would have heard some of his influence in our music.

But anyway, this is the most important confession in this book: categorically, without Paul Weller in my life it would have been significantly less rich. Here are ten reasons why:

1. The first time I heard The Jam: only a faint memory, playing 'Modern World' on cassette with my mates across the road.
2. This time paying much more attention – to the chart rundown. No. 15 with 'Strange Town', the same week as 'Cool for Cats' by Squeeze was at 2, Art Garfunkel's 'Bright Eyes' was No. 1 and The Village People, Kate Bush and Siouxsie and The Banshees were all in the charts. I still have the chart on C90 cassette – it's genius.
3. Buying 'David Watts'/'A-Bomb in Wardour Street' and taking it to the local church youth club in Davenham, where there was one record player, one record and one

DJ – me. I played both sides alternately over and over and over again, till someone went home and brought back a Stranglers record.

4. I bought everything they ever did. I have every original Jam and Style Council 7-inch and album.

5. 'Life from a Window' became my favourite Jam song ever. I used to play it before going out every night. The lyrics just seemed to represent the 16/17-year-old me so well. When I first met Alan McGee and was talking about The Jam, he said, 'You should cover "Life from a Window".' I'd not mentioned the song to him before. He had to be right – as well as many other things, McGee is a professional listener.

6. I remember wanting to show my loyalty to Weller and The Jam by dancing to 'Town Called Malice' at a school disco in Moulton. I heard the familiar sound of the Northern soul bass line and knew the dancefloor needed me. I felt a little self-conscious as people started to leave the floor, and the colour drained from me as Phil Collins's voice butted in where it should have been Weller's. I'd inadvertently jumped up to Phil's Motown-lite version of 'You Can't Hurry Love'. I had to make a split-second decision and just carried on dancing in the direction of the toilets, like when you break into a run after accidentally tripping while walking along. My dignity remained intact, and my new-found pledge to fully identify a song before hitting the dancefloor was adopted.

7. Searching for and attempting to smoke Gitanes filter-less French cigarettes à la Weller.

8. Buying a cycling top (see Weller video 'My Ever Changing Moods').

9.   Loafers.
10. The fishtail parka.

It's fair to say that Mr Weller and I are mates. I love his music. I particularly love the way he has shifted with the times. I love the anger and even the parodies.

While in Amsterdam on my solo tour, I heard he was staying in the same hotel. I dropped off my album for him with the concierge, and he called me the next day to tell me how much he liked it. I don't think he likes LA too much, but he always called me when he arrived in town.

At an Oasis concert at the Hollywood Bowl he asked me if I wanted to do a song with him the following night at the Wiltern on Western and Wilshire. I agreed, thinking we were probably going to be doing 'Town Called Malice' or 'Shout to the Top'. I was gobsmacked when he suggested 'We All Need Love' from my debut solo. I went to the soundcheck, rehearsed it with him and Steve Cradock, and performed it that night.

Later at dinner he told me I once had the greatest haircut in pop. He was always going on about my hair in a tutting kind of way. I asked when, and he said 1993–4. It was 2007. I've had many a good and bad hair day since the early '90s. Weller just found one he liked for himself some time around 1976 and has stuck with it since. There's something to be said for that.

He's now achieved the status of national treasure, but it's often forgotten that he went through some difficult times, when his music was overlooked. I'm sure there are people out there in bands who, when faced with adversity, think What Would Weller Do? It can definitely get you out of a setback.

I sometimes see the world of bands like one of those Pete Frame family trees. Before us there were Johnny Marr, Arthur Lee, Siouxsie Sioux, Marc Almond, Boy George, Adam Ant.

And after us came Mark Ronson, Factory Floor, Ariel Pink, Ladyhawke.

Ladyhawke, or Pip as she introduced herself, came to see The Charlatans at the Astoria in 2007, incidentally one of the final shows there. The aftershow party, for me and Pip at least, was the Cave Club in Islington, hosted by Spider Webb from The Horrors. It felt like home to me, reminiscent of the Manchester nightclub Berlin around 1983.

The Horrors came along at exactly the right time for me. For so long I had felt like the only person in a band that was a music nut. They were music nuts too.

Pip and I talked nonstop all night while we were listening to psyche/garage/punk 7-inch sounds until we were in a dizzy haze. We agreed that night to work together, somehow, someday. It's always beautiful when you feel a connection like that. Later, when I wrote the song 'Just One Kiss' for a project I was working on with Josh Hayward and Steff from The Klaxons, I could hear only Pip's voice.

Round about that time Mark Ronson was popping in and out of Shoreditch. I had somehow gone from young gun to elder statesman in the blink of an eye. Sometimes I would be both of these simultaneously – being introduced as 'youngsters' by The Rolling Stones while Mark Ronson told the audience tales of skipping classes to watch us in New York. Ronson was making an album of cover versions and had lined up Robbie Williams to do a song – Robbie picked 'The Only One I Know'. An album of cover versions had never previously set the world alight, but he came close to redefining it with *Version*, mainly for Amy Winehouse's take on 'Valerie'. Soon after recording it Robbie went into rehab – he was unavailable when Mark Ronson's band played Glastonbury, so I joined them to do a cover of someone doing a cover of us!

★ ★ ★

There are times when it's worth reminding yourself why you joined a band in the first place.

I first became acquainted with the unique stagecraft of Mark E. Smith at a gig at the Haçienda. He had his back to the crowd and glanced over his shoulder like an M&S Johnny Rotten, hunched up and coughing out the lyrics while seemingly oblivious to the audience. I was converted and intrigued. My friends, at least most of them, were appalled.

I last saw him in a pub in Prestwich, near to where he lived. It's something that you'd put on those lists of things you should do before you die, the musical equivalent of swimming with dolphins.

Mark has always divided opinion and always done his own thing. That's what sorts the sheep from the goats. One of Mark's biggest fans, Stewart Lee, has talked of his desire not to expand his audience but to actually hone it down to the final person, who is so like you that the two of you can go down the pub for a drink. I often think Mark has this approach.

I did join Mark in the pub, but not as his last fan. A few years earlier I'd made my way to the same Prestwich pub for that album launch party I mentioned earlier. I count it as my first music-business event after we'd started to have success with The Charlatans. It wasn't a glitzy affair.

I'd always found Mark E. Smith fascinating. Members of The Fall were parts of a machine that was constantly being stripped down and rebuilt, keeping ahead and never being associated with any particular musical fad. Everyone focuses on the fact that The Fall has had so many members, which can be a smoke screen for the sheer brilliance of their output. It's like thinking the glass is half empty rather than half full.

Mark's glass is always half full – if not overflowing.

In 2009 I'd been asked to curate a stage at the Isle of Wight Festival. The Charlatans played last on a bill that included The Horrors, Killing Joke and The Pains of Being Pure of Heart. But the first band I'd approached had been The Fall. I was told that due to other commitments they wouldn't be able to play. With Mark's infamous brutal honesty I could at least be safe in the knowledge that I wasn't being offered an excuse so as not to hurt my feelings.

I asked again in 2010 while putting together a line-up for another festival, and this time the answer was yes. A deposit had to be given to the band and I decided I would drop it off at Mark's personally: destination Prestwich, just north of the centre of Manchester. With trepidation we walked up his path, past discarded foreign coins, broken biros and spent batteries.

We were greeted by the man himself, who instantly told a tale of a recently removed exploding piano. He had stored fan mail inside it and he led us to believe that some gifts, postmarked China, had exploded.

'Seriously, in the middle of the night – BANG! Are we going up the road? Are you coming with me?' he exclaimed. Mark got the round in, one Diet Coke and three pints of Diamond, and handed us a record each. Grouchy? No! Genius? Yes! Generous? Definitely yes! That was one of my favourite afternoons in a long time. He gave us the potted history of the area and quoted long-forgotten Teutonic generals – all done in a style you could only describe as being the exact midway point between Rigsby and Gollum.

After buying the album *Perverted by Language* when it was released, I began to work backwards through the Fall catalogue: *Grotesque*, *Slates*, *Live at the Witch Trials*, *Totale's Turns*; the brilliant singles 'How I Wrote Elastic Man' and its tremendous B-side, a crackers love letter to Manchester entitled 'City

Hobgoblins' – why do you only think of words like 'entitled' when you're thinking of The Fall?

Follow this with the soon-to-become-shit-disco classic 'Totally Wired', and the lower-division terrace anthem 'Kicker Conspiracy', the 4-track Rough Trade 2 × 7-inch featuring recordings from a BBC John Peel Session – 'New Puritan' and 'Container Drivers', and a brand-new song, 'Wings', and what you have is an essential guide to early Fall, a brilliant phase of nonchalant po-faced Northern post-punk, the Rough Trade Records period spliced with a couple of sojourns at another label, Kamera.

And while we're on the subject, what about *Hex Enduction Hour* and *Room to Live*, and the singles 'Lie Dream of a Casino Soul' and 'Look, Know'.

Imagine the sound of grubby Vegas meeting Wigan Casino in pistachio green with maggots crawling inside the sleeves, and you will be close to Mark's Mark. And yes! They were incredible, concise, era-defining statements.

Here begins the story of my wonky marriage and heavy investment in The Fall.

When I first met Steve Harrison, he who would become The Charlatans' manager and for some time one of my closest friends, he had a record shop in Winsford, a Liverpool satellite overspill town. It was a 12 foot × 12 foot store facing the main road at the top of Woodford Lane. His presence was made known by the green Vespa, or was it a Lambretta?, parked outside, a little like the Queen with her flags outside Buckingham Palace. He wore an Aran polo-neck jumper and he ran the shop with his moddy girlfriend, Judith.

Steve was happy to listen to my musical musings and bag up my orders, but I often sensed a mocking tone in his voice – maybe because he was older and thought I was a little freaky fan with flawed musical knowledge. The Dead Kennedys, Section 25 and Thee Milkshakes, all bought in one go. Perhaps that would have thrown anyone. He was a bit of a music snob. I was impressed by that, though.

The Fall's 'Kicker Conspiracy' was a rambling song about George Best, the FA, Bert Millichip, some blonde girl and grotty spawn – among other things. It was perhaps my very first acquaintance with a gifted lyricist representing my feelings. A Northern, speedy rap; a sharp, intelligent and occasionally daft lyric. It had the kind of language my grandma would use, yet delivered in a thoroughly thrilling modern way like a Stretford street urchin would.

The Fall were as close to the mainstream as they would ever be at this point, signed to Beggars Banquet and making appearances on TV. But perhaps it was like a stopped clock being right just twice a day. It was time for The Fall and the mainstream to cross like some kind of visit from Halley's comet. There they were at teatime on a Friday, on stage on *The Tube*, with the latest addition to the band on six-string Rickenbacker, Brix, the new Mrs Smith. With her pretty West Coast harmonies and her sassy guitar-playing she instantly became the subject of a crush for me and every outsider teenager watching TV that night. Her addition to the band brought along a wealth of teenage men-boys, but for me it wasn't a pointless crush. I definitely wanted a band, and I definitely wanted a Brix. She would come in many forms.

Mark's lyrics and attitude, and the rhythmic blast of Karl Burns, Steve Hanley and Craig Scanlon, had been just untouchable. There was nothing to compete live and on record. John Peel christened them 'The Mighty Fall', and when additional drums were added, via Steve's brother Paul, audiences were floored.

Then along came Brix. When they got married he didn't know she could play guitar, but after he heard her play the lead, he and the band thought it worked so well that, in his own words, Mark 'went with it'. At the time, 1983, there was disbelief among Fall fans. I bet the bass player couldn't move *his* Mrs into the band.

But I suppose that's the power of the frontman. At least that's what I got out of it. He does whatever he wants.

★ ★ ★

There is often a smell I associate with a record. The Fall's *This Nation's Saving Grace* comes with the smell of grass being mown in a nearby field. Madonna's album *Like a Prayer* reminds me of patchouli oil. I thought this was just my own synaesthesia, but I found out later that the record came from the factory like that.

Most of my Crass records had a deep, inky, serious smell – kind of like some industrial odour mixed with a hint of revolution. I met up with Gee Vaucher, who made all those covers and did the sleeve for our album *Who We Touch*. I mentioned the smell and she told me that they made all the sleeves themselves, doing all the printing with paint fumes and an inky smell filling the place they worked in. It must have hung onto the covers and made it all the way to my bedroom, leaning up against my record player.

★ ★ ★

People often ask how the members of a band get on with each other after a long time together. Journalists always like to point out what they see as cracks. But they are often just lifestyle choices or down to practicalities. Simon and Garfunkel travel separately to gigs – shocker! In reality one likes art galleries and the other likes sleeping in. Last time I checked, it seemed they could each afford their own cab.

So where are we today?

Bands often answer that they are like a family. But inevitably different stages in people's lives lead to a distance that doesn't necessarily stay for good, but friendships and relationships change, compromises have to be made and the band has to remain worthwhile enough for storms to be weathered. Time away from each other heals rifts, as with The Eagles and The Stone Roses, but never breaking up has pressures of its own – pressures that are well worth enduring for the feeling that you get at the end of an amazing gig or the completion of a song.

We will meet up and travel together to a gig. We've had twenty-odd years of rehearsal and we can second guess each other. We joke around and we bicker, but we always have an eye on the bigger picture.

Our most recent album, *Who We Touch*, was overshadowed by Jon Brookes's brain tumour. Years before that, our Wonderland tour was almost abandoned after we heard Tony had been diagnosed with testicular cancer – he had been acutely aware that he was suffering from something while we were making the record but decided not to deal with it until we had finished the album – the music came before his health.

Undergoing an orchiectomy and months of chemo while touring that album was as tough as anything could be. Thankfully, Tony worked through his illness and today he is cancer-free.

Fast forward to 2010 at Johnny Brenda's in Philadelphia, seven dates into our American tour. I am singing and it dawns on me that Jon has stopped drumming. This has never happened before. I've never liked it when you're watching a band and they turn round to focus on the member who's having some trouble – a guitarist with a broken string, a singer with a dodgy mic connection. But this is what we do.

There is a curtain of twinkling beads that has become the focus of Jon's attention. He is having a brain haemorrhage.

I can't begin to comment on what it feels like, so here is Jon's own account.

Life, destiny, fate and the odds of life giving you a double dose
of diabolical luck. But the only thing I can think of is the need
to foster and nurture the future, surround it and protect it with
all the good stuff we carry in the way of excess mental baggage.

Juxtaposition is not a word which is easily squeezed into life's
patchwork of possibilities, but as I sit in the middle of the
mother of all seesaws I have the darkest blackest hole tempting
me into its featureless perpetual void, where no sounds come
and no souls stir. A place of my mind's creation, which lives off
its own power source. An energy farm of fear, a place that is
bursting with confused thoughts and random outpourings of
negative misleading ideas. A tricky place to navigate at the best
of times but to be cast into its depths weakened and disabled and
confused is not a choice I am willing to undertake. I believe evo-
lution has granted me mental freewill and I edge towards the
light and my own truth!!!

When I first saw those strange lights in the corner of my eyes
at the start of the set in Philadelphia little was I to know that the
brain tumour several centimetres across was starting to emit its
electrical impulses across the bottom half of the right hand side
of my brain . . . and after asking for sound levels to be lowered
on stage I continued to play the set, but was already hopelessly
out of time and disorientated and on a different song from the
set list and rest of the band; the countdown to disorder had
begun. Strange feelings of floating quickly replaced by violent
head movements engulfed me. Then I was approached by
strangely familiar faces asking me what was wrong but I couldn't
speak, my mouth wired tight by lockjaw and panic spreading
across my frozen body. The first seizure had begun and was in
full effect.

Time and its measurement in drum beats and rhythms and my
ability to manoeuvre it/them relative to melody and a musical
pre-determined arrangement have been my life's work. I have

also compulsively and deliberately played every concert like it's my last, but as this night came crashing down around me I felt a stillness in the room like never before, a visitor in my own world . . . my memory is patchy but I can still hear the screams of my own voice echoing out as I felt hands struggle to hold me still as I was attended to by friends and paramedics alike. The blessing is that I don't have enough recollection to be totally freaked out by the first seizure/event. And I can only feel sorry for my dear friends who had to witness such a painful display.

I was eventually brought under control and went to the nearest hospital where it was quickly discovered that another seizure was imminent and a neurological centre was the only option. It is now that I can fill in the later stages of that night. I was never frightened or concerned about my fate in as much as I knew death was not in attendance at any point, I saw no flash backs and had strong feelings of being amongst special caring people. They had a beautiful and serene calm which washed over me as I began to answer their questions and let myself be submitted to their scientific tests which seemed to involve me lying on moving platforms then entering giant polo mints . . . while offering up my arms to be pricked and probed for blood and vital signs.

The blessed relief came early on the morning of the 16th when morphine was introduced to my bloodstream to ease the muscle cramps and tears and strains of the previous night's violent struggle. At last I had time to stop and listen to my own heartbeat and the pulse that throbbed in my temple, and to grow accustomed to the hospital clothing with its random gaping, unfastenable trap doors!

The hospital was a 16-floor university campus, specializing in neuro-medicine. And I found myself attending lecture theatres filled with new students eager to investigate the new patient. It was at this point I had the first of several amazing epiphanies.

I began to realize the absolute interdependence of shared knowledge and the pure brilliance of energies exchanged in order to
investigate the chaos which to most of us is unfathomable in
such alien environments and medical situations. I had become
besieged with messages of good will from every direction, family, fans, friends, colleagues, strangers, hospital co-workers and
nurses. Baskets of fruit began to appear, comfortable clothing
was hastily packed into empty bedside tables, all sent with love
and concern. I knew that I was not alone and at the foot of my
bed, my fellow band members and road crew sat looking at me
with disbelief and sly grins from time to time, I began to feel life
was still within my grasp and thought about the option given to
me by Joseph V. Queenan, MD, Head of Neurosurgery, Hahne-
mann University Hospital, Philadelphia: 'We have located the
tumour Mr Brookes and are ready to take it out.'

I knew cancer was the main diagnosis but still had to undergo
a spinal tap to dismiss any other type of abscess. My feelings
were given over to the logistics of the immediate surgery. I had
to have my wife and kids with me in the States for the post op
but after treatment of chemotherapy and radiology I decided to
make the journey home . . . not knowing who would help me
when I stepped off the plane, I became overrun with doubt and
confusion . . . I travelled home heavily sedated with Tony
Rogers and a doctor to escort me in case of more seizures.

I want to try and explain to anyone who is interested,
the amazing power of 'positive thought' and love and light,
which can be transmitted across vast amounts of time and
space by everyone who wishes to try. I began to feel a portal
open up inside my soul, and a feeling of wellbeing charge
through me, reaching a pinnacle of absolute meltdown and
relief when I received a phone call from my dear friend Ian
Palmer telling me that Professor Garth Cruickshank had been
made aware of my situation and arranged to have me delivered

to his operating theatre . . . in the UK to remove the tumour from my brain.

I know that who we touch are touched indeed, and I will never be able to express my heartfelt thanks for all the love and light I received, from all of you who texted me, sent me cards, made calls to me or passed on their support and best wishes that ultimately brought me back home, safe!

I have the best chance of rebuilding my life now and will always have one eye on the lookout for those strange lights! But knowing that love is the key and I wouldn't be here without it . . . It is with the deepest thanks I can express that I will hopefully be back to my old self and be returned to full health with the ongoing treatment I am to receive.

I spoke to Jon in hospital, and his thoughts were all about his family and the foreseeable future of the band. We had to tour the album and Jon himself suggested Pete Salisbury from The Verve as his replacement.

Previous experiences with the band had been about where to score and I'd never given any thought to how important insurance coverage was. Like Iggy Pop, drug info was replaced by the small print of insurance policies.

Should I say that Jon Brookes is doing well and playing better than ever?

★ ★ ★

Northwich in 1982. I wasn't a prefect . . . I had myself down as one of the bad boys. Nothing too extreme – living on the edge of delinquency in Northwich at that time was more about petty shoplifting, misdemeanours with air rifles and unintentional arson. With time on our hands, a spare firework and a fabric shop opposite the off-licence in Moulton village, the three things came together in a blur of cordite and flaming curtains. I don't want to incriminate myself and, erm, Stuart Simpson, although I think the case has long since been closed by CSI Northwich.

I had myself down as a delinquent but with hindsight I think I was just a nuisance. That's not to say that some pretty serious incidents didn't occur. I always felt I had an awareness of my surroundings and my instinct would always guide me away from anything too severe. This was never better illustrated than in a proposed fishing trip with friends and their older brothers which I chose not to go on. It involved an overnight camping stay in a neighbouring village. Nothing too crazy: cigarettes were procured from parents, beer bought by those who could get served, and a camp was set up. But their antics attracted some kids from that village and a fight broke out. Foolishly, one of my friends had taken a knife along, and someone was stabbed. Five of them ended up in a detention centre for young offenders.

The only reference I had to where my friends had been sent was Alan Clarke's 1979 film *Scum*. The film was a bleak and moving insight into the kind of place they were in. But it was also a representation of the savage world we were living in. Margaret Thatcher was in power, and if anything remotely good could be said of her it was the fact that the stark times she brought with her were so cruel that people felt downtrodden enough to find a voice. Innocent men like Blair Peach and Liddle Towers were dying at the hands of the police, the IRA were bombing the British mainland, and at the same time there were huge miscarriages of justice.

The Falklands War was imminent and the dreaminess of the '60s protest songs like Dylan's 'Blowin' in the Wind' was replaced by the out-and-out reality of songs like 'How Does It Feel to Be the Mother of a Thousand Dead?' by Crass.

So there I was, 15 years old, hanging out with Leftwich High School's equivalent of deadbeats and reprobates. We were more Grange Hill than the Bloods or the Crips. I wasn't tough but I could make people laugh, and I chose to make the tough people laugh. We thought of ourselves as outcasts, into drinking and smoking. We watched videos like *The Warriors* and *The Wanderers*. And we wanted something to belong to.

★ ★ ★

So where am I today?

I am in love, I'm still a punk, I am a meditator, part of the David Lynch Foundation for consciousness-based education and world peace, and I'm happy.

I used to wonder about people whose life sounded like the kind of thing a Miss World contestant would talk about: helping other people out and generally doing good deeds. All I can say is that, for me, some kind of spirituality has replaced dependency, and I am happy. I guess I've proved that you can come out the other end.

Last week I did a speech! It's not something I'm really comfortable with, but it was a speech about transcendental meditation to a bunch of kids aged from 14 to 17. Some of them were drug-users, all of them had suffered mental and physical abuse at a school in east LA. I told them my story – the one you've read here, about my being in a band, my experience of drugs and the benefits of TM. I hope it helped them. It certainly made me feel good.

I have just got back from Nashville, where I recorded with Mark Nevers, Kurt Wagner and R. Stevie Moore. I had wanted to record with Wagner for over ten years, since I first met him in England. I met up with him in Nashville to start writing an album in April 2011.

I am writing this towards the end of 2011. I have a record label with friends and we put out music we love and I have just finished writing this book.

NO! what am I doing *right now*? I am listening to *The Great Rock 'n' Roll Swindle*, a record I bought with my saved-up pocket money from our family's first holiday in France. I bought it at a record shop in Castle, a small area of Northwich. It's now signed by The Sex Pistols' guitarist Steve Jones. He drew a cock on it.

I count him as a friend.

I am listening to Sid Vicious sing 'My Way'.

I don't feel that different from the way I did when I first bought it.

Not the End

Acknowledgements

This book could not have happened without Nic Colk Void, Nick Fraser, Sophie Williams, Tony Lacey and Simon Benham. Thank You.

To Mum, Dad and Claire – I owe you such a lot.

Manchester, Los Angeles, The Horrors, Jim Spencer, Tony Linkin.

Martin Duffy – he saved us and instilled in us the spirit to carry on.

Tony Wilson – an inspiration to a generation, much copied, much loved, much missed.

Tom and Ed – for inviting me to record with them – and to everyone who I had the privilege of collaborating with.

David Lynch – using an amazing talent to help others.

And Michelle First – you showed me some wild and beautiful times.

And the people who I've shared this adventure with, on stage and on records. We've been like brothers. We've made some amazing music and touched people's lives. For sharing this with me has meant the world: Jon Brookes, Martin Blunt, Mark Collins, Tony Rogers; Rob Collins, Jon Baker.

Finally, thanks to everyone who ever came to see us, sent us a message of support or who owns one of our records. Without this support, none of this would have been possible and for that I owe you everything.

For Where There is Love There Will Always be Miracles

Tim x